A French Adventure

A New Start at 46!

JOAN CRORY

AMBASSADOR INTERNATIONAL
Greenville, South Carolina • Belfast, Northern Ireland

A French Adventure
A New Start at 46!

ISBN 978-1-84030-198-4

Ambassador Publications
a division of
Ambassador Productions Ltd.
Providence House
Ardenlee Street,
Belfast,
BT6 8QJ
Northern Ireland
www.ambassador-productions.com

Emerald House
427 Wade Hampton Blvd.
Greenville
SC 29609, USA
www.emeraldhouse.com

Contents

1
Get Going!

We were forty-six years old . One daughter was already married and our other two children had left school well behind them when something happened which would turn our lives upside down and change us for ever. At our advanced age, my husband, George, and I were starting out on a Big Adventure. From a busy Pastorate in Belfast we had been called by God to go to France to a church-planting ministry and were stepping out into the Unknown - a bit like Abraham, not knowing where we were going. But God knew, and our lives were in His hands.

For a couple of years, we had had a growing sense that a move was in the offing. We'd had nine years of a very busy church-life, seeming like '24/7' sometimes. It had been rewarding, with growing congregations, so much so that the church had to be extended and new halls built to accommodate all the activities. It had been hard work and we had grown to love the folk there but the time had come for a change. I had thought that, in the normal course of events, George would be called to one of the pastor-less churches around us. But the days and weeks went by and nothing happened. I remained convinced, however, that we were going to move. In fact, for the first time, I hadn't bought any bulbs or plants for the garden because I was convinced I wouldn't be around to see them come up! A favourite verse of mine had always been Psalm 32 v.8: 'I will instruct you and teach you in the way you should go.' and I knew that in His own good time He would show us what to do.

In the autumn, a young missionary called Eddie came home from France, depressed, mentally exhausted and in need of a counsellor. He arrived on our door step one afternoon and asked George if he could come and talk to him. And so it was that every Monday afternoon all through the winter, Eddie would spend an hour or so talking out all his problems with George. He would stay for tea and then go home. I was never in on the discussions; I had a temporary teaching job and was out all day and would rush home to get the meal for us all.

On Monday, January 14th, it was the usual routine: Eddie called up for his counselling session in the afternoon, I was at school, with nothing more important to think about but my day with my five-year olds. George told me later that as Eddie outlined his vision for a Team Ministry in France and the need for a mature leader, it was as if the Lord said very clearly in his ear: 'You could do that …..and that ….. And that!' He said nothing to Eddie and we had tea together as usual. When Eddie had gone, George sat down and said,' I think God is calling us to France' and, like a flash of light, I thought, 'THAT'S IT! That's what I've been waiting for!' It was as clear as day and I had no doubts that this was God's plan for us. Now, we had no Bible verse to tell us and going to the Mission Field hadn't really been in our thoughts but we were convinced, right from that moment on, that this was what God wanted us to do.

George made an appointment to see our Baptist Missions secretary for the following Friday to suggest that we should go out to France under their umbrella. Then of course the Missions committee would have to be consulted and they only met every couple of months or so. It might be a long-drawn-out process, but at least we would put the wheels in motion. But life with God is full of surprises. When George explained the purpose of his visit, the reaction was quite dramatic. For one thing, the secretary was really delighted! Then he announced that the Missions committee would be meeting that very night and he showed George the agenda. The first item read: 'Prayer for personnel for team ministry in France'!! Well, if we'd been looking for confirmation, that was it. But that wasn't all. When George told Eddie that we felt the Lord had clearly told us to go, he agreed to come back to France with us as part of our team although he had been considering giving up altogether. That was really good.

The following Sunday George announced to the church that we would probably be leaving them at the end of the year to start our new ministry in France. It was as big a surprise to them as it had been to us! Afterwards we were showered with expressions of regret that we would be leaving but lots of good wishes for our future. They were dear people. That same evening, after the service a young WRAC stayed behind to give her life to the Lord. It was the first conversion in the church for a while and we felt that this was God's Seal of Approval on what we were doing.

A few days later we learnt that a friend had met a member of the Missions committee, and had been talking about us. This man took a piece of paper from his pocket which he had taken, all unknowingly, to the committee meeting. On it was written , 'George and Joan Crory as suggested workers for France'. There was really no room for doubt.

As the weeks went by, my heart began to grow heavy as I thought about our children. None of them would be coming with us. Pauline was due to get married in April, so she would be all right. Peter was about to go up to Queen's University and Fiona was just 17 and working in Belfast. But they would be losing their home. They would have no base for weekends and what would they do at Christmas? However could Fiona manage on her own in a flat and anyway flats in her price range were pretty grotty. And what about Peter? He wouldn't have any money, he'd be living on a very small grant. Many a night the tears came as I poured out my worries and concerns for them to the Lord. In my head I knew that if we obeyed Him, He would take care of the rest. Hadn't He said so? It was all very well knowing it, but I had to believe it and that was a struggle.

Then the Lord reminded me that at school in my RE classes, I had been teaching the ten-year olds that sometimes God asks us to do what might seem crazy to us or to others. Elisha and the widow, Noah, Philip and others had been the subjects of discussion. Yet in all these situations, obedience brought blessing. I had to hang on to that. It seemed hard to put our children into such a difficult situation but I had to believe that we would see God undertake for them and care for them.

Long before God had called us, George had arranged to go and visit a young couple from our church who were studying French at a language school in Paris. They were planning to go to French-speaking Africa and George wanted to see how they were getting on. Isn't it strange how God works things out? Off he went in February and took Peter with him. They returned a week later, having obviously enjoyed their visit and with George convinced that this would be a good place for us to go to in order to brush-up our almost-forgotten French. He also said that everyone there advised him that we should go at the beginning of the academic year, in September! The Lord was going to have to solve a lot of problems for us in a very short time.

Things sorted themselves out over the weeks, but by June we still hadn't found anywhere for Peter and Fiona to live. It was becoming almost an obsession with me. When I tried to pray it was the only thing I could think of. Peter left to go to a Youth Camp in the USA for a couple of months and after I'd had a good cry at the thought that I might not see him again before Christmas, I opened my Daily Light and asked the Lord to have SOMETHING to say to me. It was June 4th and at the top of the page I read: "The glory of this present house will be greater than the glory of the former house …And in this place I will grant peace." I knew this really had nothing to do with my situation but it gave me immense comfort. I felt that God was in charge of my children's housing problem and I needn't worry myself about it. Incredibly, that same lunch-time one of the parents who came to collect his daughter from my class, and who knew our situation, had news for me. A friend of his was letting two little terraced houses just off the Lisburn Road in Belfast. Maybe we'd like to go and look at them? George and I went and looked. One had been lived in but the other was in process of being totally renovated: new kitchen, new bathroom and would be furnished! We took Fiona down to see it and she felt it would do well. It was the end one in the terrace so Peter could park his old car right outside the door. It was very close to bus-stops and it was right beside the shops. And so it was that the Lord rebuked my very weak faith.

On July 1st, Fiona moved into No.2 Hugh St. It was to be the start of a big change for her; she had so much to learn about everything but she was very resilient and abundantly cheerful and we knew she would make the best of it. Peter would be sharing the house with her so we were happy about that: they were good buddies.

On September 2nd we had a Farewell evening in the church. Peter had returned from America earlier than expected, so we were all together. I was afraid it might turn out to be a weepy affair and was specially anxious for our children but, thanks to the Lord, we had a lovely evening with a few laughs. We were given gifts from the various groups in the church. George was presented with a glass owl paper-weight from the diaconate and the deacon who presented it said he felt that the white face and the bags under the eyes would be a constant reminder of office-bearers' meetings! There were so many people present, all wanting to wish us well. Specially precious were the kind friends who promised they would look after our family.

A couple of days later we had our last meal together as a family in Fiona's little house. She had gone to great lengths to make everything nice for us and it was very hard to keep the tears back. But all good things come to an end and we hugged them all for the last time. We would be leaving for France the following morning.

2
BACK TO SCHOOL

Our first stop was to be language school in Paris and that's where we were heading on September 5th,1985. We took the ferry from Rosslare and the skies got bluer and the sun shone brighter all the way. Normally I would have loved it but darkness was dawning on my soul as the emotional stress of the past few weeks began to catch up with me and I developed a thumping headache. The night passed and I slept fitfully in my bunk, trying hard not to think about the children.

Awaking to another beautiful day, I was forced to spend most of it horizontal. The fears crowded in: how would Peter and Fiona cope? How could they possibly pay all the bills? They'd never had to do all the housekeeping before, how would they manage? Desperate prayers ascended to the Heavenly Father accompanied by not a few tears. Even George's excited report of seeing dolphins frolicking in front of the ship failed to move me.

Leaving the boat at Le Havre, a 5-hour drive brought us to our new home for the next nine months, language school. By the time we arrived, we were both physically and mentally exhausted. Lugging our cases up seemingly endless flights of stairs to the flat allocated to us on the top floor, tears threatened. Looking around the two rooms which were to be our living quarters for the best part of a year didn't improve the situation. We felt 'basic' was maybe too generous a description! There were no cups, no fronts to the two cupboards, stains everywhere, ghastly un-ironed curtains, with not enough curtain rings, drooping at the windows and all electric plugs were hanging off the walls or attached with Sellotape. We dumped our cases on the floor, sat down and looked at each other. It wasn't exactly a 'home from home'. "How on earth are you going to survive in this place?" whispered the devil in my ear. The room was hot and stuffy and smelt a bit stale and my heart sank even further. We couldn't even make a cup of tea!

"Right," said George, ever the optimist, "Come on. We have to go and buy milk and tea and a few other things to keep us going." So we dragged ourselves up, down all the stairs again and out to find the nearest shop to buy the wherewithal to keep body and soul together.

By bedtime I felt quite at the end of any resources I'd ever had. Sick at heart, tired to death, anxious for the children and just a bit apprehensive about all that lay ahead. But the Everlasting Arms were still underneath even though I hadn't the strength to search for them. I slept fitfully and woke to a new day.

Sleep is a great healer and as I looked out and saw blue skies and sun, my spirits began to lift. George rearranged what little furniture we had, put up photographs and pictures to cover most of the stains and things began to look up.

Despite such an inauspicious beginning, language school proved to be a great experience. There were fifty-five students from seven or eight different countries all training to work for the Lord in Francophone areas of the world. We found it really stimulating. We had to sit tests to assess the level of our French and right from the start absolutely every word spoken in class was in French, not one word of English! Help! It was a shock to the system, but oh, so good for us. Our French lay at least thirty years in the past and we had to work really hard to dredge it up! Although it was September, the temperature was still in the high 20sC and our little flat was hot. Even with all the windows open, the heat was stifling and it was hard to concentrate on homework and writing exercises when one's hand stuck to the page!

Living in our flat forced us to be exceptionally tidy. Everything had to be replaced within a centimetre of where it had come from or there was no room for it. There was only one 40w light bulb in the room, hopeless for working, so George bought a 100w bulb to lighten our world. When he unscrewed the old one, the entire light fitting fell off the ceiling. Hysterical laughter saved us from despair! And so, little by little, we got used to our new surroundings and even began to enjoy them.

My readings from Daily Light were a constant source of comfort and encouragement to me. As I read them each morning, I was assured of God's love for me, for George and for the children. Just a week after our arrival in France I read: 'I will give them singleness of heart and action so that they will always fear Me for their own good and the good of their children after them.' Jer.32;39. So long as we kept our eyes fixed on the goal of serving God in France, doing whatever it might be that He had called us to do, all would be well with us, and with our family as well. The main thing is to keep the main thing as the Main Thing, as the man said.

Not being at all 'au fait' with French shops, the supermarket was a real eye-opener. It was HUGE, with young assistants on roller skates flying up and down the aisles, stocking shelves and missing the customers by inches. The fish counter was a picture, very artistically arranged. It even had octopi spread out, showing the suckers all down their tentacles. Ugh, do people really eat them? Above the oven-ready chickens were packs of what looked like four little sparrows neatly arranged in a row, (we discovered later that these were quails), there were whole rabbits, still wearing their furry feet, and the most amazing cheese counter we had ever seen. Much to our own surprise and that of our family, we became avid blue- cheese-lovers over the years, which we would never have become in Belfast. We had no idea what some of the foods were that we were looking at : it seemed that food was going to present another learning curve.

Occasionally, after a busy day of study we would take the metro and go into Paris. What a beautiful city it is! We loved it in the evenings. There was a magic in the air, with the Eiffel Tower lit up and looming out of the darkness. We enjoyed just strolling around listening to the buzz of French conversation from the folk sitting outside the restaurants and just breathing in the atmosphere.

One evening we decided to take a trip down the River Seine on a bâteau-mouche so that we could see the sights from a different angle. Once on the boat it was announced that we couldn't follow the normal route because barriers had been erected on the river, so we went the other way. And what did we see? - cement works, ducks and a few 1960's era bridges and that was all! To add insult to injury we were then invited to buy a trashy green Eiffel Tower or a 'Vive la France' hat! Cheek!

In between these treats, we worked hard. Temperatures were still in the 20'sC in October and it was hard to write essays with sticky hands. But we persevered and began to make progress. The teachers were really good and we enjoyed their classes. The student body was great and we began to make some special friends.

We had opportunities to meet 'real' French people from time to time. We began to teach English once a week to 14-yr old Olivier. This we really enjoyed although it's quite hard to teach one's own language. But he was bright and intelligent and learned quickly. The lessons opened the way for us to meet his parents, Yolande and Michel. We invited them to tea in the flat and were able to hold a conversation with them. They were very friendly and we got on well together. We had been thinking that it would be a good idea to buy a TV to help us to learn about current affairs and to 'tune our ears in', but prices were prohibitive. We asked Michel if he knew where we could buy a secondhand set in good condition, at which he smiled broadly and announced that he worked for Phillips TV!! The Lord had been there before us! So before too long we were the proud owners of a nice little set which proved to be a real asset in helping our comprehension of 'La Belle Langue Francaise'.

We had constant reminders of God's good care of us. One of the most wonderful was an offer from a gentleman in N.Ireland who invited us to go to his furniture store the next time we were home to choose all we might need for our new home! How kind God's people are: we never ceased to be amazed at their generosity and interest in all that we were doing. This was an answer to prayer before we'd even thought to pray! "He knows what things you have need of before you ask Him," Jesus had told His disciples, and we were proving the truth of it.

Each term the language school organised an outreach team in answer to a plea from a church needing help. We always volunteered to go and it gave us a good insight into church life in France. The first one was in Rouen, a very historic old town. We were lodged in the beautiful old house, (built in Napoleon's time,) of one of the church members. The walls were three feet thick and there was a lovely walled garden surrounding the property.

On the Saturday afternoon we went into the town centre to sing and give out literature inviting folk to a film service that evening. One or two church members came with us, as did the pastor. I moved off with the literature group and the others grouped themselves in front of the shops. Only a few minutes had passed before we became conscious of a lot of shouting. A young man, a street singer, had approached our folk, really angry, saying that they had taken his pitch. To prove his point he snatched a guitar from one of the girls and started to sing, with the Christians standing behind like his backing group. I hoped he was singing something decent! Then he stormed off, and after a moment of prayer the singing re-started.

But we hadn't seen the end of him. Back he came, armed with a bucket which he proceeded to fill from a tap in the street. He then swooshed the water all over the pavement at the singers' feet. Bravely they sang on. (It was beginning to look like a comic opera at this stage.) By this time quite a crowd had gathered and were having a lively discussion about the rights and wrongs of the affair. We literature distributors seized the opportunity and handed out dozens of leaflets. It's an ill wind...... Some of the folk tried to reason with the young man, but he was beyond listening. In a furious temper he re-filled his bucket and this time threw the whole contents right over the singers. Some of them, including George, were absolutely drenched.

The pastor decided that enough was enough and we moved off to try and find a less exciting place to witness. We left behind us a lot of animated discussion and a very wet pavement. At least we had made an impact! Re-arranging ourselves on the steps of a large church, we started again. But perhaps God wasn't welcome in Rouen that day, for no sooner had we sung a few lines than the singing was drowned in a mighty roar as about a hundred motor cycles came hurtling up the road, engines roaring, to stop just opposite us. The noise was incredible and it was impossible to think, let alone sing or speak. Apparently two bikers were getting married in the church behind us and this was their support group.

This convinced us it was time to go. We'd made ourselves known, maybe not exactly as we had intended; we'd given out lots of invitations and for George and me it had been something of an eye-opener. If we hadn't known it before, we knew it now. France was going to be different. But God was in control and we left matters in His hands.

Another memorable weekend in our first term was spent in Villefranche. We had links with the church there as Eddie, a young man who had been working with them was preparing to come and join us when we left language school. We stayed with a lovely couple who did everything they could to make us welcome. After a weekend of talking French practically non-stop and meeting the folk in the church , we thought it would be nice to buy something for our host and hostess. So we went out to look at the shops but everything was far too expensive for our rather limited means. And then we came upon a flower-shop just bursting at the seams with the most beautiful chrysanthemums. The very thing!

We bought a pot of stunning blooms and proudly presented it to our hostess on leaving. We thought she looked at us rather oddly but she thanked us and we left. Only much later did we discover that the following day had been the Festival of the Dead and the chrysanthemums were exclusively for putting on graves for the Dear Departed and not, definitely NOT for giving to the living! To her eternal credit, she said not a word. Oh dear, our first real faux-pas. No doubt it wouldn't be our last!

During that weekend, the pastor had taken us on a tour of the area to see if we could get an idea of where we would like to settle. We saw lots of little towns and villages, all of them with no evangelical witness of any sort but the Lord said nothing. We would have to wait.

Being separated from the family was a constant ache, so imagine our joy when we returned to Paris to find that Fiona was planning to come over and stay for a week. We were so excited, getting ready for her. It was such a blessing to see her, well and in good spirits. She was enchanted by Paris, as we were. We talked non-stop and the week flew by all too quickly. We shed a few tears at having to say goodbye again but our prayers went with her. It was only a few weeks before we would be home in Ireland for Christmas but in between were the dreaded exams!

We worked hard, learned all our subjunctives and irregular verbs and burnt the midnight oil. Happily it paid off and we both got over 80% in all the papers. Relieved and feeling very pleased with ourselves, we prepared to pack our cases.

Would it surprise you to know that things did not go smoothly for our journey home? The day before we were due to fly out, we heard that Charles de Gaulle airport would be closed on 20th just for the day because of a strike. Typical! Frantically we rang British Airways who said, "If you get to the airport for 8.30am we will provide a bus to take you to Brussels and we will fly you to Belfast from there." What a palaver!

So, it was up at 5.30am on the 20th and a quick walk with our cases to the metro station. We arrived just in time to hear an announcement: 'There will be no trains at all today because of strike action!' So there we were, in the dark, 7 o'clock in the morning and no way of getting anywhere. George tried to phone for a taxi - no taxis. Nothing to do but pray. And out of the darkness came an unknown French girl, saying, 'Do you want to get to Paris? Wait there while I go and get my car." The Lord works in mysterious ways. She drove like the clappers and dropped us at the Gare du Nord at just on 8 o'clock. George flew over to the taxi rank and asked the first driver if he could get us to Charles de Gaulle by 8.30? Answer? - 'No way, much too far.' Help! George then made up his mind to ask all the taxi-drivers and the second one agreed. We flung our cases in and he drove as the French are reputed to drive, getting us there with just five minutes to spare. We threw him a hefty tip and tore inside only to learn that there would be no bus, but if we waited, an extra plane was being put on for 11am and that would get us home. We sat down, ordered a coffee and marvelled at the way God works things out.

Our first term at language school had certainly made an impression on us. We'd had a few troubles and trials but we had learnt such a lot, not just the French language but more importantly about our Heavenly Father's provision for us.

In January, Margaret arrived from Belfast. She was planning to do six months of study and then she would join us to be part of our missionary team. As it happened, language school proved to be really much better than she had imagined: she fell in love with a young American missionary and the romance blossomed before our eyes.

As the weather warmed up we spent more and more time in the garden. 'Garden' did I say? It was a bit of a dustbowl with scrubby grass struggling to exist There were a couple of washing-lines strung under the trees and the inevitable volley-ball court at the far end. In April the table-tennis tables were brought out and many a raucous hour was spent watching matches being fought in front of amazingly partisan onlookers. It was all great fun and good relaxation.

The rest of the year flew by. Our cramped little flat gradually became a meeting-place for students who toiled up the stairs to ask for help with their studies, or even for advice about their love-life!! Lots of them came just for coffee and a chat and we had a few hilarious evenings playing games. Even a few of the teachers dropped in now and then. It was really good and we enjoyed having Open House

The end of term was drawing very near and we needed to find out what the next step was going to be. We already knew by experience that God never shows us the next step before the time is right but there was no harm in pushing doors. So George spent a weekend in Villefranche again talking to the pastor (and preaching in the church!). He asked if the pastor would look around the area for properties to rent and he agreed. That might be a pointer.

At the end of May we became the owners of our first French car. It was a Citroen GS, about five years old, and we had passed it often on our way to the metro station and had noticed the For Sale notice on it. George had begun to think we might enquire about it. After a day or two, he plucked up courage and went to see the man, offering him 3000F, (about £300), which was a couple of hundred francs less than the asking price. It was left for the owner to telephone us if he wanted to accept that. Two days later the phone rang - the car was ours! Once again the Lord had undertaken for us; the price was almost exactly what we had sold our car for in Belfast , and so we could afford it. All we needed was to learn to drive on the wrong side of the road, and in Paris, of all places! It was a bit of a daunting prospect.

Our friendship with Yolande and Michel, the Phillips TV man, blossomed during the year and we had a good conversation one day about the Holy Spirit, who He was and what was His role. Yolande asked me to write out a few Bible references for her to look up and I did so. When the end of term arrived and they came to say goodbye, she said they were going off on holiday and that she was taking her Bible and was going to look up all the verses I had given her. We never saw the family again but prayed that the seed of interest that had been planted in her heart would one day bear fruit.

Then in June the Lord provided us with our new home. George got a phone-call one day from the pastor saying that a flat was being held for us to view in a town called Trévoux. All it needed was for George to go down and see if it was suitable. The town was somewhere between Villefranche and Lyon and George set off the next day. That evening he rang, very excited, and said, "It's the home of our dreams. You'll really love it!" That was wonderful and the future looked rosy

It was sad to say goodbye to all the friends we had made at the school but it was with great anticipation that at the end of the month we piled all our belongings into our car and headed south. It was a long way, about three hundred miles, and it was HOT, at least 30C. Strangely, we hardly noticed it. Our expectation was high. What did the Lord have in store for us this time? We had no idea what lay ahead but we were supremely confident that we were in His will and that He would fulfil His plans for us. As yet we had no furniture but we did have a lovely flat, which I couldn't wait to see. There would be new acquaintances to make, and new opportunities for service. God had provided everything we needed during the year and we knew we were safe in His care. We drove on towards our new home. This was what our year of study had been preparing us for and we were really looking forward to our new life. It was yet another step into the Unknown.

3
Getting Started

Arriving in Trévoux from Paris, it was dark. At 10pm it was still amazingly warm; the night was very still, the silence broken only by the chirping of crickets – a sound which ever after brought an immediate reminder of France. We drove up to our building: lights on in a few windows, three or four flats in process of completion, half a dozen cars parked neatly along the sandy driveway. Not a sound!

Our flat was on the first floor. We climbed the steps and opened the door to our new home. A fairly spacious hallway with doors opening off it: bathroom, toilet, two rooms for bedrooms and a room with nothing but a sink unit, obviously the kitchen! We were the first tenants so everything was very clean. Lovely tiled floors everywhere, bliss for walking bare-footed! Nice. Facing us were two glass doors. We opened them and WOW! – a huge room with a smaller one opening off it. Two large windows in walls three feet thick, overlooking the garden; a massive stone fireplace and a really old wooden beam across the ceiling (300 years old, we learned later). From a corner of the room a pine staircase led to a lovely mezzanine – like a minstrels' gallery – and a large upper floor. It was spacious and airy and wonderful!

Early the next day we went out to buy a few provisions and to explore this little French town which was to be our home for who knew how many years. Trévoux was a lovely little place of about 7000 pop. built high up above the River Saône. There was a town square with a little bandstand in the centre and a large Catholic church on one side. The Mairie, or town hall, was on the side facing the river and there were stone benches under the trees where one could sit and watch the world go by. From the square a zigzag path led down the slope to the river which flowed majestically down to join the Rhône at Lyon.

One main street of small shops led to the Old Quarter – every French town seems to have one – where many streets dated from as far back as the 13th century. There was a steep set of well-worn, uneven steps leading down to the 'lavoir', a huge stone tank of water where some of the Arab ladies still did their washing. This descent was very aptly named 'rue Casse-Cou', which being interpreted means 'Break your Neck Street'! It was quaint and picturesque and I loved it on sight. I felt like the Psalmist when he exclaimed, 'The lines have fallen to me in pleasant places!' This was certainly a 'pleasant place'.

"God was so good to us in those very early days", reflects George. "I had left a busy church behind in Ireland where I was able to use my gifts to the full in my own culture and language. Now the position was reversed – I could speak only the simplest of French phrases and was back to being a 'learner' again in the truest sense with all the nervousness and insecurity that went with it. Joan on her part had found it very difficult to say goodbye to our children and launch out into the unknown but our God is compassionate, and He brought us to this truly lovely little town where we might find rest for our souls and prepare for the first steps of the ministry for which He had sent us to France in the first place. Our Lord had given us the grace to obey his call back in Ireland and now we were beginning to understand what was meant by those words in 1 Sam. 2:30: "'Those who honour me, I will honour'".

Eddie and Margaret both moved in with us so we needed all that space. For a month we all 'camped out'. We had no real furniture, just mattresses on the floor and folding garden chairs to sit on and a two-burner camping stove. It was great, no housework to do and time to get to know each other as a team and to pray together about the future. We did, of course eventually have to buy a washing-machine and fridge and a few cupboards for the kitchen but they didn't come all at once. We lived out of boxes.

Our little TV helped us with our French and we needed all the help we could get. Language school had been really good for teaching grammar but we soon realised that we didn't know how to say the simplest things. I occasionally met one of the neighbours from the flats beside us as I hung out the washing on the communal washing-lines in the garden. After an initial "Bonjour, Madame!", I would find that I had absolutely no idea what she had said in reply. It was so frustrating. Everybody seemed to talk so fast!

We began to discover new and different things about our way of life ; every morning we trekked down the long drive from our flat to the gate where a dozen mailboxes were fastened to the wall. We had a key for ours and always opened it with great expectation. Letters were a treat! They were delivered by a post girl who drove up on a little yellow motor-bike which loudly announced her arrival each morning. If the box was empty, we felt ridiculously let-down.

It was not the 'done thing' to call on someone without giving notice and certainly not after about 7 o'clock at night.

People worked long hours, getting home late and we discovered that our neighbours tended to put on their pyjamas as soon as they arrived home and then ate their evening meal. So they certainly didn't want callers.

In August George travelled over to Ireland to arrange for all our furniture to be brought over. There were endless forms to fill in; the French just love their paper-work! And we had heard stories of people not being allowed to bring in furniture that had been bought within the last six months. There were all sorts of import rules and regulations and we just hoped and prayed that we'd got it right. We had asked folk at home to pray our furniture through and we were trusting God to work things out for us.

The day before George was due back, Margaret, Eddie and I travelled up to meet him. We had a scare on the way up to Paris: a stone shattered our windscreen as we overtook a van, and for a few moments we couldn't see a thing and we were in the fast lane! We managed to get off it safely with nothing more than a few tiny cuts from flying glass, but we were pretty shaken. Then we had to find a garage who would effect the repairs. Eventually we were off again, none the worse but a few hours later than planned. We spent the night in the language school and that awoke lots of happy memories. We even found one or two students still flitting around the place. That was nice and then it was bed and an early start in the morning for the long drive up to Calais to meet the boat.

The lorry duly arrived – with Fiona aboard! – and then began the long wait for Customs clearance. We were told we hadn't got the correct forms. More waiting. Lots of praying. Five hours passed and then with no warning we were told we could go, with no search of the lorry, no tax to pay and all our goods intact! Well, once again our prayers had been answered. It really was a miracle.

Fiona stayed with us for a month, revelling in the hot sunshine and looking like a Red Indian after only a couple of days. It was so good to be with her. Things were quite difficult at home for her and she had been unable to find anyone to share the house with her and Peter in order to help with the expense. But she was her irrepressible self and quite philosophical about it. We were the ones who worried. We explored the surrounding area a bit and discovered a couple of places that were to become firm favourites in the future. One was a Bird Park where a huge stretch of parkland housed all sorts of exotic birds from the far-flung corners of the earth. It was beautifully laid out with lots of trees and lakes and plenty of room for picnics. Two or three hours passed quickly as there was so much to see. The other 'find' was a mediaeval walled town called Pérouges. Cars were not allowed inside the gates, the streets were narrow, twisty and cobbled; tiny little shops hid themselves between the houses and it was literally like stepping back in time. No telephone cables to be seen – all modern wiring was underground so as not to spoil the illusion. There was a lovely old Hostellerie and one could almost believe that the four Musketeers would suddenly walk in! We always ended our visits there with a drink of hot chocolate and a slice of 'Galette', a sort of very flat sugary bread. Delicious!

By the end of August we had found flats for both Margaret and Eddie. We helped to get them established and then set our minds to establishing ourselves. Soon the furniture was all in place, the boxes were empty and stored away and it looked like 'home'. Another task we had to perform was to arrange for the delivery of all our winter fuel – logs, not coal. With some of the neighbours, we ordered a lorry-load which arrived a few days later. We watched as the lorry came slowly up the drive, piled high with two feet-long lengths of wood which were then just tipped out into the middle of the drive. We paid the driver and off he went, leaving an immense pile of logs behind him. Then it was all hands on deck for a couple of hours, dividing the load into piles, one for each of the neighbours and after that stacking it into a little shed under the steps up to our flat. Oddly, in years to come, our delivery of firewood always seemed to arrive on a baking hot day and sorting it out proved to be a really exhausting job. For George, the worst bit was that we had a huge resident toad who lived in our shed and would be sitting just inside the door each time we opened it!

As a team we met often to pray and make plans for the future. How did we begin? We knew nobody in the town, certainly no other Christians, so what were we going to do? We travelled the 20kms to Villefranche on Sundays to worship with the church there and began to get to know the church members. Several of them were keen to support us in whatever we decided to do and they encouraged us by their interest.

With Eddie and Margaret out of the flat, George and I began to realise just how drastically our lives had changed. Up until this point, we had had people with us all the time. At language school we had been surrounded by all sorts of people and had hardly had a moment to ourselves, and before that, back in Belfast we had been so busy with church activities that we had hardly seen each other. If George had had a night in, I was out and vice versa and we were virtually on the go all the time. But now all that was finished and here we were, just the two of us together, all day, every day. We found it very strange, and sometimes, quite difficult. We almost felt guilty because we weren't rushing about any more. No meetings to go to; for George no hours in the study preparing; for me no days at school, teaching, and dashing back to get meals before the evening rush of activity.

I took to walking! I walked the length and breadth of Trévoux, exploring all the little streets and finding out where they went. Often I would walk down the hill to the river. There was always something to see, little boats going up and down and the occasional 'bâteau mouche' taking a party of friends down the river to Lyon. Their voices and laughter would float across the water and they would wave cheerfully as they went by. If I was feeling extra-energetic, I would walk to the next village. The streets would be quiet in the summer heat and practically deserted, just the occasional dog would bark a couple of times as I went past, and then flop down again on the doorstep. There would be the sleepy drone of a tractor working in the fields and I would pass a sea of sunflowers, their faces up to the sun and beside them, fields of maize plants. It was always calm and tranquil and balm to the soul, and in those days of just starting off I really enjoyed soaking up the beauty of this lovely country.

George's salvation was the garden. He had always loved gardening, especially the 'creating' stage, and he had plenty of scope for that! We had asked the landlord about having a garden when we first moved in. Apparently none of the other tenants had shown any interest so he pointed out a slope of ground just inside the gates and said we could have it. Well, it was obvious that no-one had ever done anything with it before. It was covered in brambles and tough clumps of grass and bits of bushes. The soil was practically pure sand, full of stones. George, the Lion-Heart, got going. He dug and sweated, raked and generally attacked with vigour. Gradually the slope got cleared and then the next job was to terrace the whole area so that we could sit there, and have our table and chairs out.

He levelled an area right at the top of the slope and sowed it with grass seed. That would be our sitting place. The weather was dry and hot so we had to water it often. After a few days we went up one morning to see if there were any signs of life and to our amazement we found all the grass seed had been neatly gathered into little triangular heaps at intervals round the edge of the square. ANTS!! There were hundreds of them solemnly marching about our precious 'garden', lifting a grass seed apiece, and depositing it in a designated spot. For a while we watched them, fascinated. How organised they were! They really were wonderful little creatures, but never mind that, they were ruining our lawn! So we re-sowed the seeds (several days running) and eventually they took root and began to grow and we watched with pleasure as the green haze became a lawn (not an English-style velvet carpet, but good enough!)

Then, down to the next level, a nice rockery separating the two and then a few nicely-raked soil beds for our vegetables. Over the years we grew hundreds of tomatoes, warmed by the sun and full of flavour, and lettuces and various other things. A crazy-paving path wound up the slope from bottom to top and under the mulberry tree on the other side George made a patio where we would keep the barbecue. By the time he had finished (this didn't happen all at once!) it was a real picture and we were very proud of it. The other tenants loved it too and one couple asked if he'd create something for them on a little scrap of ground behind the cars.

We got involved as much as we could in the Billy Graham Crusade which was being relayed to Lyon. A few folk from Villefranche were converted and that was encouraging. We resolved to start a Bible Study in Eddie's flat on Tuesday evenings. Three or four folk from Villefranche promised to come but we hoped that before long we'd see someone from our own town joining us.

We realised that we needed to make ourselves known in the area and in the end took the decision to do three major tract distributions 10,000 tracts each in Trévoux and Neuville, which was the next sizeable town, and all the little villages in between. We chose our tracts, drew a collective deep breath and ordered 30,000!

At that point George and I had to leave and go back to Ireland for our first-ever period of Deputation, giving reports on the work to all the churches who supported us. In six weeks we travelled over 6000 miles, and spoke at fifty-one meetings from Sunday Schools to a meeting with the whole student body at Belfast Bible College. By the end of it we were well and truly exhausted but had been impressed by the warmth of the welcome given to us personally and the level of interest in what we had to say about France.

We stayed with Pauline and David but only saw them late at night when we returned from a meeting . Even so, we often sat up late talking with them and even playing games until the wee, small hours. It was good to be with them. We didn't see much of Peter and Fiona, just now and then when we could fit it in but they were fine and getting on with life. What we didn't know was that Fiona was planning to go to London with friends and to find a job there. We only discovered that just before we left for France again. We weren't too happy about it but her mind was made up.

While we were away, Margaret and Eddie had really got into the swing of things. The Bible Study had got off the ground with a regular eight or nine people, Margaret was helping with a Sunday School class in Villefranche and had joined a lace-making class, and Eddie had had some good chats about God with a couple living beside him. The tracts had arrived and were waiting to be stamped with our name and telephone number. We planned three separate distributions from December to February and hoped we would get a good response.

On our return, we felt that our French had deserted us a bit and we needed to find folk to talk to. We started by inviting the neighbour from downstairs up for coffee. She was a young woman called Marie-Annick and was very open and friendly. This was to prove to be the beginning of a long and lasting friendship with her and her husband, Gilles. We also invited one or two friends from the Bible Study group to come for meals in our flat where we had to speak French for two or three hours at a time. Sometimes it was really hard-going and we always ended these evenings with a headache but it was the best way to improve. I'm not a specially good cook, and to begin with, I generally panicked about what to serve to these French folk who were all so knowledgeable about 'cuisine'! But then I had a bright idea – serve up an Irish meal: Irish stew followed by apple tart and custard! Easy, and that's what I did until my confidence increased and I began to try other things.

We spent hours stamping tracts and eventually started the distribution. It proved to be quite an experience. No going up the path to the front door and putting a tract through the letter-box here! Practically every house stood behind locked gates and it seemed that everyone in the area was the proud owner of a really fierce dog. They ran along the fence as we passed by, splitting our ears with their barking; they growled at us as we looked for the elusive mail-boxes which hid themselves under the ivy on the wall or behind the pillars at the gate or just round the corner from the house. It became a race to get the tract into the box before the dog caught up with you! At one house there were three salukis lurking in the garden. I had just reached the mail-box at the gate when one of them came tearing down the drive, took a flying leap at the gate, reached right over it and bit me on the shoulder! I nearly died of shock and my heart was still thumping hours later. I toyed with the idea of going back and asking for compensation for my ripped jacket but decided that wouldn't be a good idea. Anyway, I'd never get up to the front door!

In spite of all that, I really enjoyed being outside and drinking in the beauty of the little villages. These little leaflets were going into homes of people who had probably never heard the Gospel and we prayed each one on its way. One thing that spurred us on in our distribution was the fact that out of 35,000 towns and villages in France, over 30,000 had no evangelical witness whatever. At least we were reducing the numbers by one or two!

The Lord began to bring new people across our path. An elderly couple stopped to talk to George one day when he was outside working in the garden. He told them who he was and why he was living in Trévoux. We realised that the whole town knew we had arrived. After all, we were the only British people living there. This was underlined for us when we received a letter in our mail-box one day addressed to 'The Pastor, Trévoux'!! A few weeks later this same lady arrived at our door. She had problems that she couldn't cope with alone and she told us she had decided to 'go and see the pastor'. That doesn't seem very odd to us, but for a French person to do such a thing was really amazing. They are usually very wary of strangers and not at all in a hurry to get to know foreigners. So we felt that God was in it.

After talking and praying with her we told her that we were hoping to teach English and, within a week or so, her granddaughter, Elodie, arrived to make arrangements for lessons. She was accompanied by her father, Alain, who sat and talked for ages. At one point he said to George, "You're a Pastor, aren't you? Can you tell me the difference between a Protestant and a Catholic church?" Well, what a question! It was such a thrill to sit and tell this man about salvation by faith and to see him really taking it in. This was why we had come to France.

Christmas loomed, although you would never have guessed it in Trévoux. Not a Christmas tree in sight, no carols in supermarkets, not even a Christmas card on sale anywhere. The French did not 'do' Christmas! On November 30th we got our first Christmas card and soon they were arriving in dozens. We Blu-tacked them up our stairs and anywhere else we could find a space. Our flat began to look really festive.

We felt we needed to do something for our neighbours, so we sent invitations to everyone in our building (by this time there were about five flats occupied), asking them to a Soirée Irlandaise in our flat. Eddie asked a couple of his neighbours, too and to our amazement they all accepted. Some of them we hadn't even met! George and I made a quick trip to Marks and Spencer in Lyon and bought a Christmas cake and some mince pies, - unheard-of in Trévoux! Fourteen people turned up. We had a buffet supper and then showed a few slides of Ireland. We sang some carols, in English, and read the Christmas Story from Luke 2, explaining that this was what made Christmas important to us.

It all went really well and afterwards they sat on and talked until about midnight ; very late for France! One lady thanked us and confided: "I've never spoken to any of my neighbours before tonight!", so we felt we had done some good for community relations in our building. Many of them exclaimed about all our cards and someone asked if we kept them from year to year!

This had been a very interesting year for us. In many ways our lives had changed – it was so different from home. We had also gleaned a lot about this beautiful country we were living in. Although surrounded by beauty, the French were not a very happy people; they complained a lot, and they consumed more medication than any other people in Europe (so we had been told!). A French friend had told us a joke, against himself really: "When God was creating France, He really went to town. He made majestic mountains and beautiful beaches, wonderful flowers and wide, flowing rivers and he gave it a lovely climate. When He had finished, He considered what He had done and wondered if maybe He had been too generous.....so He created the French!!"

What else had we learned about our adopted country? – The influence of the occult was very strong; mediums and fortune-tellers abounded. It had been calculated that there were 48,000 astrologers in the population compared to 42,000 medical doctors.

There existed little or no Christian influence: evangelicals accounted for less than .1% of the population. In Lyon, France's second biggest city, there was only one Christian bookshop for one and a half million people. 80% of French people had never owned a Bible and 45million people had no church connection. Religion was not allowed to be taught in schools but Philosophy was a compulsory subject. Consequently it was very difficult for Christians, very often isolated and without much support. In fact 15-25% of missionaries left after their first term and 28% dropped out before they had completed ten years. So we knew we weren't going to have an easy road but we seemed to have made a good beginning and we felt that the year 1987 had ended on a fairly high note. What a lot we had experienced in just a few months: frustrations, thrills, fears and expectations. Above all we had been very conscious that this was where God wanted us to be and that was exciting. We looked forward with anticipation to the New Year.

4
Making Progress

The New Year brought us good news on the family front. After six months of unemployment, Peter had at last found a job, albeit temporary, in a haulage firm. Fiona had gone to London to work, and wrote assuring us that she was happy and enjoying her job in a large hotel. And then Pauline rang: "Good news, Mum – I'm expecting!" and the baby was due in August. That was really super news; imagine being grandparents! At least we had a few months to get used to the idea. On top of all that, I learnt that a favourite cousin of mine whom I had lost touch with on leaving London 25 years ago, was now living and working in Grenoble, only two hours away! That was a thrill, and we were able to arrange to meet again and catch up on all the lost years.

At the end of the month we prepared to start our second major distribution. This time we included details of our Tuesday Bible Studies and also offered English lessons. It was COLD! Not only did France have proper summers but we discovered that it had real winters, too. We were amazed to see blocks of ice floating down the River Saône and huge icicles hanging from every projection on the buildings. We bought snow boots. Mine were grey with orange streaks and George's were blue with yellow stripes! Out we went into the snow, not the one-inch-deep-soon-to-be-grey-slush type of snow we were used to, but dazzlingly white, crisp, beautiful snow about six inches deep. It blanketed our world and transformed it into a real Winter Wonderland.

After only a week, we actually got a response. It came from a young man who lived in Trévoux. He said that he and his wife were recently converted and didn't know any other Christians, so had been delighted to get our leaflet. Could they come and see us? You can imagine our joy! We arranged a meeting with the team and Jean-Charles and his wife, Grazziella, duly arrived. They had come to know the Lord when on a visit to S.America and were now looking for fellowship. Gladly we told them all about ourselves and they promised to join us. That was a thrill!

Our Missions Secretary arrived for a week's visit and we involved him in everything we were doing. I quote from his report:

'Perhaps the most exciting moment of the week was the Bible Study on Tuesday night. This was to start at 8pm but at 8.25pm there were still only ourselves. Then one after another they arrived until Eddie's flat was packed with 17 people. Three were unconverted, one was a new Christian who had been contacted through the tract distribution (that was Jean-Charles), and a number were young, struggling Christians. A few believers had come from Villefranche to help. The discussion was on knowing God in a personal way. Eddie's expertise enabled him to involve everyone in open, honest discussion. George, Joan and Margaret displayed real sensitivity and joined in significantly at vital moments. Everybody contributed.

People turned to their Bibles. It was just like a New Testament situation in the Early Church where we were reasoning from the Scriptures. The Lord's presence was so real. Brigitte, Christine and Pascal, (the three new-comers) displayed an obvious hunger for the truth. Pray for them, especially Brigitte who asked, "If there is a God and He is good, how can I get to know Him?"'

This had been the first occasion that we had changed our normal Bible Study format to a debate. It was exciting to see the new girls there; Eddie had met them a few days before with a friend of his from Villefranche and invited them along. They seemed genuine in their desire to know more, admitting that they weren't even sure that God existed. From then on they came regularly every Tuesday and we could almost see the light dawning as the Holy Spirit opened their eyes to see the truth.

By now we were teaching English regularly three times a week and Margaret had got a job teaching in a local school a couple of afternoons a week. Our circle of acquaintances was rapidly widening and we began to feel the need to find premises where we could establish an identity. To rent property for any activities all groups had to register with the authorities as an 'Association' of some sort. We couldn't advertise ourselves as a church , we weren't – yet. So we called ourselves the 'French-Irish Evangelical Association' and deposited the necessary papers, lots of them, with the local authority. We also began to haunt the estate agents' offices looking for somewhere suitable.

We had decided that Neuville would be a good central location. It was quite a prosperous little town about the same size as Trévoux but with much more life about it. It dated from about 7ooAD and had never had any established evangelical witness at all. We walked around it and it really felt 'right'. We looked at one or two properties but none was suitable. We were prepared to wait for the Lord to find us the right place. There was no hurry.

In March we felt that the time had come to commence a Sunday evening worship service. We would hold it in our flat twice a month and see what happened. Alain, who continued to accompany his daughter, Elodie, to her English lessons, was fast becoming a good friend. George asked him one day if he would like to come and join us on the following Sunday night and he immediately agreed. And come he did. The fact that he was the only French person there with us four Brits didn't seem to faze him at all. Afterwards we offered him a Bible which he readily accepted and promised to read. Was the seed falling on good soil? We hoped so.

April proved to be quite a month. With Eddie away in Ireland on Deputation, it fell to George to take charge of all the Tuesday nights. That meant a great deal of preparation and prayer. A discussion can be tricky enough to lead in English, let alone in French and as yet he didn't have Eddie's fluency! But he did very well and the ones and twos began to join us, brought by our 'regulars'. A young Arab man called Chahab seemed to really appreciate being part of the group and always had penetrating questions to ask. He asked me one night, "Does the Bible have anything to say about Forgiveness?". I assured him it did and wrote out a list of verses for him to look up. We had given him a Bible earlier and he went home seriously intending to make a study of them. There was a real need there, and we prayed that God would meet it.

We were increasingly conscious of our need to learn more of the language but as yet had not been able to find any suitable classes to join. Then in April we got a phone-call from the Chamber of Commerce in Villefranche where we had made enquiries, saying a course would be starting soon and would we be interested? Indeed we were and for a whole term we spent two hours every Friday increasing our facility in French. It was a weird course, lots of singing and music, but it did help a bit.

It was a bad month for me – I had my first-ever car accident in thirty years of driving! It was a pouring wet morning and as I approached the traffic lights in Trévoux, the car just took off when I braked, (aquaplaning?) and I slammed hard into the back of the car in front. Horrified, I flew out to see if the occupants were hurt. They weren't, but the car wasn't so fortunate! The occupants were Italian and I could barely make out their heavily-accented French!. I did however deduce that they had just had their car repaired in order to sell it that afternoon!!! Not having a clue what to do, I persuaded them to accompany me home where I hoped George could work out the intricacies of the matter. They came and he did. They stayed for a cup of tea and we parted on friendly terms, even having arranged to meet again for tea during the following week! All's well that ends well.

Time flew by and our days were well filled. Soon it was time for our third distribution, this time offering a copy of John's Gospel with each tract. So far we had given out 20,000 tracts and had only two or three replies. Undeterred we set out again and by the end of May had had not one reply!

As the weather got warmer we spent lots of time in the garden with our neighbours. Nearly always the conversation came round to what we believed and why. Our special friends were Marie-Annick and Gilles from downstairs and a German couple called Katarina and Matthias who lived next door. These were a very musically-talented young pair who played in one of the orchestras in Germany. Katarina and I soon formed a good friendship and she would come up to the flat once or twice a week and we would play our way through Bach and Chopin and Mozart, me on the piano and her on the flute, often with her year-old son clinging on to her leg! We loved it and it really brought us very close. It was so refreshing to talk about our faith to folk who genuinely wanted to know and to whom the Gospel was something new and interesting.

These contacts kept us on our spiritual toes and drove us ever closer to the Lord. We needed His help as we endeavoured to introduce Him to everyone we met. It was challenging and exciting.

We continued to miss our children but had the joy of seeing both Peter and Pauline who each came to stay for a week. Pauline was seven months pregnant and there had been some concern about her flying but all went well and she enjoyed her first look at the Saône valley. She was in good health and looking forward to the arrival of her baby. Apparently Fiona had decided to leave London and go back to N. Ireland now that she was going to be an auntie. That was good news, as was the fact that she intended to come out to us for the month of August. Peter had a new job: he had just been appointed General Secretary of a YMCA. Thank you, Lord. That's right up his street.

In June we found our premises! A building was vacant right in the heart of Neuville. It comprised a shop front with two large windows on to the street, a huge filthy space behind which had been some sort of workshop and was black and greasy everywhere, and a flat above. Apart from the state of it, it was perfect. The Mission gave us the go-ahead and the lease was signed – a few dozen times, à la francais! This was a big step forward but there would be hours and hours of scrubbing and cleaning to make the place half-decent in order to start holding our activities there. The lease was signed and we were told we could take possession in September.

As if in confirmation that this was the right step, we got a phone-call from a young woman, a direct result of the May distribution. She was a Christian and lived in Genay, which was Eddie's village, and said if we had a group she would like to join it. Then George and I were in Neuville market one morning giving out leaflets. The market was a hive of noise, bustle and colour. About a hundred stalls were set up on what was usually a riverside car-park. There was a vast array of goods for sale: clothes, vegetables and fruit in abundance, a stall selling nothing but baskets of all shapes and sizes, hats, underwear – everything! There were huge trailers housing meat and cheese counters and stalls selling olives and oysters and all sorts of shell-fish. A long queue of people carrying plastic water containers waited beside a white van. What on earth were they buying? It couldn't be petrol; surely it wasn't water? Indeed it wasn't. They were buying their week's supply of ....wine, being dispensed from vats in the van via hosepipe!! This wasn't vintage Bordeaux or Chardonnay but just their ordinary table wine which France consumes in gallons. Above all was the hum of voices, the constant kissing of both cheeks as folk met their friends, greeting them loudly and every now and then the penetrating voice of a stall-holder shouting his wares. The air was permeated by the inviting aroma of 'crêpes' sizzling on the hot plates. It was the vibrant, pulsating heart of the town – a good place for missionaries!

We were there giving out leaflets advertising our arrival in the town and stating our beliefs. I handed one to a young woman who walked away, reading it carefully. After about half an hour she came back and said she was really interested in knowing who we were and would like to bring her husband along to meet us. We invited her to our flat for an evening and they duly came. It transpired that they were Christians, called Florence and Michel, who had belonged to a church near Lyon which had split and closed down. Since then they had had no church to go to and once they had quizzed us on what we believed, they felt happy to join us. They said that there was at least one other family who would want to come, too. And between them they had nine children!

We had just got our premises and now the Lord was bringing us a ready-made congregation – and a Sunday School! It really was quite amazing. The following Sunday they all arrived at our flat in Trévoux for the worship service. We were quite a crowd. The children were lovely and very well-behaved and seemed happy to be there. As they were leaving, Michel said, "If you want them, there are thirty chairs in our garage which belonged to our last church. They're not being used, so you can have them if you like."!

That summer we had our first Summer Team from N.Ireland with us for a fortnight. We had a busy programme: mornings spent in Bible Study and Orientation; afternoons spent in distribution of invitations to the activities; evenings with barbecues, Irish nights, films and other outreach events. The young people were enthusiastic workers but found it hard to cope with temperatures in the 30sC. Giving out literature exhausted them! One poor girl returned after an afternoon of treading the streets, with wrists and ankles really swollen by the heat, and headed for a cold shower! We invited all the contacts we had and were thrilled to have about 20 unconverted folk in. We hoped that when September came we'd see many of them coming into our regular church activities.

The team had only just left when we got a phone-call to say that our very first grandson, Mark David, had safely arrived. What a thrill, but how frustrating to be so far away! His other granny rang to say how lovely he was and that nearly made it worse. There was no way I could stay away any longer, so within a week I had packed my bags and flown off to see him. He was as gorgeous as had been reported and I spent a very happy ten days oohing and aahing and thoroughly revelling in being a granny. Sadly the time passed far too quickly and I had to return to France but there was work to do and I needed to be there.

Brigitte and Christine continued to attend the Bible Studies and were beginning to understand more and more of the truth of the Bible. We felt they were very near to accepting Christ into their lives and we waited for the day to come with great expectation. One Sunday Margaret invited them both to her flat for a meal. Eddie was there, too and they talked a great deal about what being a Christian was all about. It seemed to settle all their queries and after a couple of hours both girls got down on their knees and asked the Lord to come into their lives. That was a very special moment and a huge encouragement to all of us.

Margaret went off for her holidays and came back glowing and with a sparkly ring on her finger. She and Robert had got engaged and had set a wedding date for March. We were delighted for them both but sad that it would mean that Margaret would leave us . She would be going to Grenoble where Robert was working with the Unevangelised Fields Mission. That would leave a big gap in our work; Margaret provided the music for all our activities. That meant I would need to learn how to play the guitar, and quickly. Margaret offered to give me lessons and after weeks of very painful finger-tips, I began to get the hang of it.

In September, work started in earnest on our premises. What a job! The place was a mess! We washed and scrubbed the shop part of it and began to hold our Sunday and Tuesday gatherings there. It was a bit noisy with all the traffic going by, and we felt a bit exposed but at least people would know we were there. We took care to have really eye-catching window displays on a theme, eg Autumn, Marriage, Sheep etc. and always printed out an appropriate Bible verse to be displayed prominently. We were well aware that for many passers-by that would be the first time they had ever read anything from the Bible. It was noticeable how many people stopped and looked and then raised their eyes to our sign above the window to see who we were. It was generally accepted that we were a 'sect'.

Autumn came, and to prove the point, the temperature dropped from 30C to 20C all in the space of a week. The fields were full of maize ready to be harvested and the trees began to glow red and orange. September brought us two outstanding events in the life of our little group. The first one was Brigitte's baptism, our very first one! She had been doing really well and knew that for her this was the next step. Her parents were scandalised and flatly refused to come to the service but she invited about ten of her friends, none of whom had ever experienced such an event before. They all came and on a warm September Sunday, after the church service in Villefranche, we all trooped down to the River Saône. We sat on the banks and listened as the Pastor simply explained what was going to happen and what it meant. Then Brigitte walked into the very muddy waters of the river where Eddie baptised her. She gave a clear, unwavering testimony of her conversion and it was a very moving moment for all of us.

The other important day was the opening and dedication of our premises. A friend from Villefranche told us that the American astronaut, James Irwin, would be in the area and he felt sure would be willing to do the honours. That would be extraordinary, Neuville would really have to take note! Within the space of two weeks we had organised a buffet meal with goodies from the local delicatessen,(not having any idea how many would be there!), and had given out invitations to the mayor, local dignitaries, the local priest and anyone else we could think of who had any influence in the town. We couldn't do very much to improve the premises in such a short time so we covered the walls with red, white and blue crepe paper and hoped the dirt wouldn't show through. We advertised the fact that a real, live astronaut was coming to inaugurate our humble little premises – a concept scorned by many in the town. We heard it rumoured that folk were saying we would just have a cardboard cut-out!

James Irwin was a lovely, humble man who did the honours beautifully. He talked about walking on the moon and said that walking with God was even more important. All the folk we had asked came, more curious probably to meet this famous man than to meet us, but no matter. The Mayor brought the town's Golden Book for James to sign, and everyone there was given a copy of his book 'More Than Just an Earthling'. There were about sixty folk there and we had a super day. That had certainly put us on the map, and we praised God for the way that so many things had fallen into place to make it happen. Once again we felt reassured that this was where God wanted us to be, and things seemed to be going well. Was it too good to last?

5
Ups And Downs

We seemed to live in a permanent dust-cloud! Work had begun in earnest on our premises. Margaret had left us to do her six weeks in Ireland and was then staying on to prepare for her wedding in March. So the next time we'd see her, she'd be floating up the aisle! That left me, George and Eddie to get started on the Grand Demolition.

We attacked the place with vigour. Walls came down, and the rotting staircase; the room behind the shop gradually became a mountain of bricks and plaster, grey dust covered everything, including us and we drove back to Trévoux every night filthy and exhausted. Windows needed to be replaced and the French wiring system proved to be totally beyond comprehension. We needed help and sent out an urgent appeal to the churches in Ireland: 'Come over into, not Macedonia but Neuville, and help us!'

They turned up trumps and before long two electricians arrived and then a couple of joiners. They were wonderful! We got the rubble cleared away and before long a transformation occurred. They certainly had a will to work and would hardly stop for a lunch break. A lovely pine staircase was built and installed, new floors were laid, windows put in and a lot of plastering and painting done.

In the midst of all the dirt and dust we carried on our normal activities. A new couple joined us – Francoise and Nicolas. She was slim and smiley, obviously glad to have found a new spiritual family; he seemed a bit aggressive and suspicious. We put it down to initial shyness and welcomed them both.

The Bible Studies had settled at a steady 15-20 folk and were really good. We would sit round in a circle, someone would make coffee and off we'd go. Whatever the subject happened to be, there was always lots of participation. The French just love a debate and sometimes they were so keen to get in on the discussion that we had to call a halt and ask them not to speak all at the same time. Time was not really important and quite often the meeting would go on for a couple of hours.

We started a special project in March when we bought a box of Bibles at a very competitive price and brought them with us one Tuesday night.

"Right, everyone, we want to ask you to join in with this special effort. Here we have lots of Bibles and what we want is for everyone here to buy at least one and to give it to a friend or neighbour who hasn't got one." Would they respond? we wondered. To our delight, twenty were bought and given out in just one month so that was very encouraging. Needless to say we had to do it ourselves as well.

I went into the shop next door to our centre and offered a Bible to the lady there. "Oh," she said, "Do you know, I've never had a Bible in my hand before!" She was about fifty years old and accepted it gratefully and said she would read it. We also gave a copy to Marie-Annick and Gilles, our friends in the flat below us. Like most people we knew, they never went to church but they took the Bible and years later, when in their house one day, we saw that same Bible sitting on the bedside table!

Lynette was the wife of a local vet and had started regularly coming to everything. She was a very hospitable lady and invited us for a meal to her home one evening. The table was beautifully laid and there were appetising smells coming from the kitchen. As usual we sat around and drank aperitifs for half an hour or so before moving to the table. First course? – snails!! Horrors! She laughed at our dumbfounded expressions and explained that seeing we were newcomers to France, it was only right that we tasted the French specialities. We had no idea what to do with them so we watched everyone else. Pick them up with a cocktail stick and suck! Right, it was shut your eyes and grit your teeth time. Actually it wasn't as awful an experience as we had feared. They were extremely gristly and chewy but tasted of nothing except the garlic butter which covered them. Even so, we were very glad when that course was over. Next course? Paella with mussels, lobster and quails – another first. George and I were not too fond of shellfish but actually it was delicious. No meat and two veg here! After all that we had a delicious dessert washed down with coffee. As is normal in France the meal lasted about three hours with lots of conversation between courses. We had to learn to eat slowly; the French are never in a rush when there's food on the go and I have to say we learnt to greatly appreciate this new rhythm of life.

Money from Ireland bought us a new minibus and in March we two, Eddie and a few French friends piled into it and set off for Calais. We were off to Margaret and Robert's wedding and were really looking forward to a welcome break from Neuville

for a little while. The crossing was awful- a full-blown gale
raged as we crossed the Channel. It was practically impossible
to remain upright and after a while we took to our bunks.
George, Eddie and I shared a cabin and every now and then
one of us was grabbing for the sick bag!! It was horrible and
didn't let up the whole time we were on the boat. We staggered
off the other end, glad to be on terra firma. Waiting to meet us
were some of the folk who had agreed to give hospitality to
our French friends. Introductions were made and off they
went. We hoped they would be able to make themselves
understood!

We were staying with Pauline and David and wee Mark so
that was a treat. And we made an effort to see Peter and Fiona
as often as we could. The wedding was lovely even though it
snowed a bit, and the bride was radiant, as brides always are. We
met up again with one or two students from language school so
that was very special as well. While we were home, friends from
our own church gave us two carpets and an electronic organ for
our centre in Neuville. We were rather overwhelmed and also a
bit apprehensive thinking about those awful French Customs.
Would we get them through? You know the answer to that : we
were waved through with no trouble at all – Oh, we of little
faith!

Arriving back in France we got the good news that a young
lady in her 20s, called Julie had been seconded to our team in
Neuville for a year. She would arrive in September. Great! That
would fill the gap left by Margaret.

Very soon Eddie left for his turn in Ireland and that meant
there were only the two of us. It also meant that all the preaching
and teaching and a great deal of the renovation work was up to
George. And it began to take its toll. He started to show all the
classic signs of stress: he didn't sleep well, he had constant
headaches and flashing lights in his eyes; he became irritable

and didn't want to talk. In fact I got really worried about him. There was no help in sight, really.

But just when it seemed that things were going seriously wrong, the carpenters came back for a second session, and they proved to be life-savers for George. The burden of all the physical work was lifted and he was able to concentrate on preparing his sermons and studies. They were great 'craic', as the Irish say, and that worked wonders. We laughed together and had great fun in between working and they were a tonic. Lots of outstanding jobs seemed to get done by magic and our centre took on a new look. The room behind the shop, which we intended to use as our 'church' looked lovely and our spirits lifted. I was so grateful to the Lord for solving that problem!

Then we met the Davidsons. They arrived at the centre one afternoon in June, looking for a group to attach themselves to. They were Christians and had been in France for four years. The lady, Marion, told me that they had joined other groups in the past but had been badly treated by them all and so had split with them. That didn't sound good but we said they would be welcome to join with us for worship. So they came and all seemed well.

Our 'church' was clean and bright and all ready when our second Summer Team arrived, and it was in the Davidsons' garden that we held our Barbecue and they welcomed over forty people to it. They supported our outreach nights during that fortnight and seemed to be settling happily. In September Julie arrived, very excited to be part of our team and full of enthusiasm. She had been teaching in a Nursery school at home and was keen to start a Children's Church and a Good News Club. So she planned and prepared and Marion offered to help her. Our newcomer, Francoise said she would like to get involved with the children too and we were happy to agree.

We felt all was going well until one Sunday, after the morning service, Marion came storming down from upstairs saying , "I can't go on like this! It's impossible to work with these people!" We were totally shocked and couldn't get any sense out of her. We asked Julie and Francoise what had happened but they had no more idea than we had. In the end we concluded that she wanted to be in charge of whatever was going on and didn't appreciate being just one of the helpers. She was totally unreasonable and stormed off home with her husband in tow.

That left us all with a sinking feeling in the pit of our stomachs. Things had been going along so smoothly up until then. Later that week George and Eddie went to see the two of them but found that they had decided that we had treated them badly, just like all the rest, and they were not coming back. That was a sad episode and our hearts were a bit sore, for them as well as for ourselves.

Meanwhile there was work to be done in Neuville. We took another step forward and began to have a Breaking of Bread service on Sunday mornings. We always had a time of open worship during the service and it was a time when practically everyone there took part. Even the little ones would pray. One little girl, called Alice, aged 5, discovered that she loved praying out loud and it got to the point where she was praying three or four times! So I had a little word with her, and suggested that maybe just one prayer would be a good idea!

George and I had advertised English Classes and we began with ten students. I took the Beginners and he took the more advanced students. It was hard work, sometimes but great fun. For example:

Joan: "Good afternoon, Eric."

Eric: "Er….yes……'Allo!"

Joan: "How are you?"

Eric, after a long pause for consideration, "Um.....I am find."

Joan: "No...fine, Fine!"

Eric, looking worried: "Oh. Am fine....yes." and so on and so forth. But we persevered and we got there, or nearly got there.

We did not evangelise during the classes. The students had paid to learn English and that's what we did for an hour twice a week. But when the class was finished, we usually had a coffee together and that's when the questions started : 'Where do you come from? Why are you in France? What else do you do beside teaching English?' And we told them. As the years passed these folk became very good friends and many of them came to the services or special Christian events that we held.

Problems were now beginning to hit our 'regulars'. Two of our ladies, Lynette, the vet's wife, and Martine had been really upset by members of their own families who were Jehovah's Witnesses and who were actively opposed to our little group. Many of our folk had had dealings with the JWs and their teachings and with no Biblical background to fall back on had become very confused. We were constantly meeting this sort of problem but when it came from members of the family it was even more difficult to counteract. We really felt our need of wisdom and understanding in these circumstances.

Alain, who was so involved with us right at the beginning had disappeared from the scene. His work-hours had changed and he could no longer meet with us. We had missed him. He had seemed to be making such good progress in understanding about the Lord. We hadn't seen him for about a year, and then, out of the blue, he turned up in Neuville one day. It was so good to see him! He came into the centre and sat and talked to George for ages. We invited him to come to our services on Sundays but he didn't promise.

November 16th was the anniversary of the opening of our premises and a young man was converted during our morning service! What a thrill! The sad thing was that he wasn't a Frenchman; he was a Scot who was over on holiday just for that week! Nevertheless we were delighted to see the Lord at work and felt really encouraged.

Eleven people responded to a leaflet we had given out offering a copy of John Blanchard's book 'Ultimate Questions' and we had the joy of going to these homes to deliver the books and were able to have good conversations with folk. One request came from a man who came into our centre one afternoon. In his hand he held a rather grubby leaflet that he had found in the street. He had read it and seen the book offer, so came in to claim his copy!

During the year it had been borne in upon us increasingly that for French people, commitment to church was a foreign policy. On their list of priorities it certainly wasn't No.1 and seemed to be about No.30 – not for all of them, but for the majority. So we sent out a letter to our most regular folk asking them to come to a meeting with us. About 15 letters went out and on the night how many turned up? Five: Martine, Lynette, Brigitte and our 'new' pair, Francoise and Nicolas. We told them we were looking for whole-hearted support from 'Active Members' who would not come just if it suited them but who would be there with a full heart to support the work. At the end of the evening, Nicolas said he and his wife would definitely not be signing up to anything; Brigitte was already there, she had been very faithful all along; Martine and Lynette both said they wanted to become involved but for them it would mean baptism, and that was a huge step for both of them to take. So, although we sometimes had 30 or more people at our Sunday service, in fact there were only three ladies willing to give us their full support. That hit us quite hard, but we just had to accept that things would not be easy. We were breaking new ground here and had to expect difficulties. God never promised us an easy path, but we knew He was there with us.

But we ended on a high note. Dec.8th came round again, the 'Open Doors' fete in Neuville. All the shops stayed open until about 10 o'clock, many of them with their wares spread outside on tables to entice folk inside. Not to be outdone, we decided to make a splash, too.

Julie and Lynette spent hours preparing colouring competitions and invitations to a Good News Club for any children who came in. We made sure that our shop shelves were well-stocked with books, Bibles and other literature. We asked our friends to help, and on the night we had folk ready to make crêpes on a little stove and to serve hot drinks. We prayed for the success of the evening and were so pleased to see our premises filled with a jostling crowd of folk eager to taste the 'Spécialités Irlandaises' (that meant traybakes and pancakes which we had been busy baking). The crêpes were snapped up as soon as they were cooked and people spilled into our church room where Eddie had set up a very good exhibition explaining who we were and what we were doing in the Saône Valley. All the colouring sheets were taken and Julie and Lynette looked forward to having a good crowd of children the following week at the Good News Club. We managed to sell one Bible and a few pieces of literature. Tired but satisfied we cleared up and went home. It had been a successful evening's effort.

When the day of the Good News Club dawned Julie and Lynette were ready nice and early. They had bought and wrapped twenty little gifts for the children who came and had prizes for the competition. At three o'clock they opened the doors and no-one came! They waited about fifteen minutes and eventually about four little children turned up. Rather disappointed they welcomed them in and sat them in the front row. A Child Evangelism Fellowship worker had agreed to come and speak and he had a lovely presentation of the Christmas story all prepared. Out of the four little ones only one of them had ever heard the story before, so seed was sown on good ground and that had to be worthwhile.

Once again Christmas was almost upon us. George and I were going to Ireland to celebrate with the family. We really felt that we had earned a bit of a break this time and looked forward to being back with all that was dear and familiar to us. Looking back on it, we had been through a year of ups and downs. Truly, we never knew what a day would bring forth. Here we were at the end of our third year in France and we had no idea what the next twelve months would bring. Would they be better or worse? There was no way of knowing.

6
Hard Times

After a really good Christmas in Ireland with family and friends, it was time for our tour of the churches again. As usual we were touched by all the tokens of interest and affection but after five weeks of meetings practically every night we were absolutely worn out. Thanks to the generosity of kind friends, George and I were both offered the chance of a week's break: George to a cottage by the sea and me to Cornwall to visit my mother aged 86 and to see my only sister and her family.

We both appreciated the break immensely. George needed to recover his enthusiasm and a solitary week with nothing to do but sit in the conservatory and look at the sea just yards from the front door, or to take long, solitary walks along the deserted beach, this was balm to his soul!

I was so happy to be with my folks in beautiful Cornwall. It was February and there were no tourists thronging the streets as there always are in the summer and we had the place to ourselves (figuratively speaking!) My mother was very well; independent as ever, in her 80's, running around giving a helping hand to the 'old folks' in the town!! The week was a tonic and George and I felt renewed and refreshed.

For the first time ever, though, I had been having misgivings about going back to France. Usually I looked forward to it: I loved the beauty of the country and the way of life; I had generally enjoyed all our new experiences in Church-Planting but I just had niggling anxieties at the back of my mind. Perhaps I had a premonition that there were tough times ahead?

To begin with, all went well. The Neuville folk seemed genuinely glad to have us back and Eddie and Julie thoughtfully gave us a week off to get settled back into our French life. It should have been a relaxing week, but the day after returning to France we had to turn round and drive all the way to the airport at Lyon to pick up a man who had offered to come out for a week to help with a few outstanding jobs in our centre. We didn't really feel ready to have a guest for a week, but we appreciated his offer and welcomed him into our home.

But oh dear, he turned out to be a very difficult guest. He showed absolutely no interest in what we were doing and sadly we came to the conclusion that he was just after a free holiday. He insisted that we take him to Geneva one day despite our pleas of other things to do. The irony of the situation was that, once on the motor-way, we got caught up in the most awful traffic hold-up and were stuck for about an hour. In the end we just turned round and drove all the way back home. That did not please our guest who locked himself in the bathroom and lay in a hot bath for a couple of hours in a sulk! For the rest of the week, he complained about most things – even the sheet on his bed was too short! He did do a little bit of work, but the end of the week just couldn't come quickly enough for us, or for him! So that was a sad little episode and we felt really disappointed.

Things in Neuville were encouraging. For the first time ever, George was able to sit one Sunday in the service as a member of the congregation, and take no part at all in the proceedings. French folk did the lot, even to welcoming people at the door. That was a real step forward. Brigitte was noticeable by her absence. She was working at the PTT (Post Office) and worked really anti-social hours, sometimes not leaving work before 7.30pm and then she had to eat, so no way could she come to anything in the evenings. The sad thing was that she hadn't put in an appearance on Sunday mornings for months. We were really anxious about her: people can so easily just slip away.

Preparations were afoot for a Thanksgiving Weekend in April. Julie's pastor and a friend were coming to speak; there was to be a church meal on the Saturday before a service of praise, and then on the Sunday we planned to have the very first-ever service of Believers' Baptism to be held in Neuville!! That was exciting. The only problem was that we didn't have a baptistry and nor did anyone else within reach! Now, how could we solve that problem?

We hit on the idea of going to a local firm of swimming-pool makers and asking them to help. It was quite funny, trying to explain what we wanted i.e. a portable baptism tank. They had no idea what we were talking about. "How many people are going to be in it at one time?" they asked. We assured them, only one, and in the end they caught on and produced a bright blue heavy-duty plastic tank. It looked like a rather long bath but would do the job perfectly. Our home church in Belfast had generously offered to cover the cost so all was well. We had no hot water system in the centre, but that was just another hurdle to be overcome on the day.

We had thought there would be three candidates: Francoise's son Emmanuel, Lynette, the vet's wife, and Martine.

They were all very serious about their commitment, and Martine especially had had long talks with us about getting her life straightened out. When we first met her, she was living with an unbeliever and she had began to have doubts about that. We talked a lot about the Biblical view of sex and marriage and after a lot of heart-searching she asked him to move out. There was quite a lot of hurt over the situation but she felt she had done the right thing.

A few weeks before her baptism, she arrived at the service with a new man in tow. Jean was about sixty, a very sprightly little man showing great interest in what was going on in our centre. Martine told us how she had met him: she had advertised in the Lonely Hearts column of the newspaper and had prayed that God would give her a Christian!! The French certainly have a novel way of doing things! Jean wasn't a Christian but she never stopped talking to him about her faith. He came to all the Bible Studies and on Sundays too and much prayer went up for him.

The week before the Baptismal service proved to be a trying one for the candidates. Francoise said that Emmanuel was being really difficult at home, Lynette told us she nearly phoned us to back out and she had invited the local RC priest up to ask if he thought she was doing the right thing!! Martine rang Julie, feeling depressed because Jean was having doubts about all he had been learning, and so on and so forth. We felt that the sooner April 16th dawned, the better!

It did, eventually. The centre looked lovely, full of flowers; the meal was laid upstairs and the chairs were all in place for the services. Saturday went well with a good crowd present, lots of singing and several new people in. It all augured well for Sunday …. We woke to pouring rain! Oh dear, let's hope that doesn't put people off. George and I were down in the centre early. The baptistry took pride of place at the front of the room and we got all the pots and pans we could find and began heating water to fill it! Everything went wonderfully well. The candidates were five, not three, and fifty-five people crammed in to watch, for many of whom this was something totally new. Each candidate told why they were taking this step and there were a few tears shed. There was no doubt that for each of them it was a momentous decision. The Lord's presence was so real you could feel it, and we, as a team, were really thrilled to see the evidence of God's work in the lives of these dear French folk.

The meal was a huge success, crowned with an enormous cake from the pâtisserie in the shape of a Bible, covered in marzipan and chocolate, filled with strawberries, cream and sponge. It was truly delicious – and must have cost a fortune! It was a gift to the church from the folk who had been baptised. Jean stayed and ate with us but left quickly afterwards and went for a walk, looking very perturbed. He had a lot to think about.

A couple of weeks later, he came into the centre one afternoon and said he wanted to talk to George. Off they went upstairs to our Prayer Room and they were there for hours! But when they came down, Jean's face said it all. He came bouncing into the shop where I was changing the window-display: "Joan, I've something to tell you. George made a lovely prayer and I have asked the Lord Jesus to save me. So now I am part of the family, too!" He was so excited and gave me a big hug and a kiss á la francais, and then did the same for George! What a thrill, and isn't God good! We rejoiced together for a little while longer and then he said he would like to tell everybody at the service on Sunday. We agreed that would be super and off he skipped to go and tell Martine. She'll be so happy! We rang Eddie and Julie to tell them the good news. There was a lot of rejoicing going on!

Over the years we had come to realise that Christian work in France was often one step forward and six steps back. Just as things seemed to be advancing, the devil would throw a spanner in the works and cause us to feel discouraged. The baptisms had been a high point but very soon afterwards, Lynette disappeared from the scene. We knew her husband had been opposed to the step she had taken and that her family had been unhappy about her association with us. It's not easy to follow-up people in France. They don't appreciate you calling at their homes and feel their business is their own affair. So we waited. Brigitte had not made an appearance for months and some of the other folk who normally were quite regular in attendance would suddenly stop coming, without any obvious reason. Two or three months later, they would turn up again, with no explanation, and behave as if nothing had happened. We found it quite hard to cope with. It was certainly discouraging.

Coming into the summer, we planned a Church Weekend away, in a Youth for Christ centre. Lots of folk said they would come and we anticipated a good time of getting to know them all much better. As the date neared, one by one they dropped out for one reason or another, and in the end we were just twelve. That was another let-down, but in the end we had a very good time. The weather was hot and we were glad of the swimming-pool. We had good times around the table studying the Scriptures and discussing all sorts of issues. God was with us, and on the last night gave us the icing on the cake: Lynette's 15-year old daughter asked Jesus into her life, all alone in her bedroom. She was going to need the prayers of all of us – she would be the only Christian in a school of 2000! That was just a lovely end to the weekend and we all came back, glowing with the thrill of having seen the Lord at work in another life.

Julie and Eddie started up a Youth Group on Saturday nights and had half a dozen young people who attended. They played table-tennis and had talks and discussions and we were glad to see things going well for them. Most of them were from our church families but occasionally a new face would appear and we prayed that the work would grow.

At the end of the month we felt the time was right to again challenge our folk to become 'Active Members' of our Association. This time we were delighted to see a real difference in attitude. Last time only three had 'signed up' but this time there were twelve who wanted to commit themselves to the work. We were especially pleased at the changed attitude of Nicolas who was so much against getting involved the last time. He and Francoise were proving to be two of our most faithful supporters.

The encouragement of that evening was offset by the ongoing saga of Martine and Jean. Things had not worked out for them and it seemed the break-up point was approaching. There was a great deal of bitterness on both sides and it seemed distinctly possible that we would lose them both. Martine had told him it was over between them and he refused to accept it, became very bitter and started telephoning the church folk, complaining that Martine was after his money! As a result she took off to the South of France and we saw her no more. Months later we heard that she had invited David back again, the man she was living with when we first met her!

Our experience as a group in Neuville was becoming a bit of a roller-coaster ride! One minute we were up and the next we were being plunged into disappointment. We began to wonder what on earth was going to happen next. Well, it was good news from home this time: Peter rang from Belfast to tell us he had just got engaged, - to another Pauline! We knew her slightly and were really pleased to hear that the pair of them were planning to come and spend a week in Trévoux during an Inter-rail tour of Europe. It was hard to have to miss the goings-on in the family. We would like to have been there for his 'courting' days! We heard that he had gone down on one knee on a leafy roundabout in the middle of Belfast to propose. How could any girl refuse!!

Before going off for our summer holidays we had a stream of Irish visitors coming to stay. It was always super to have them in our home and to catch up on all the news. One dear friend had been to stay more than once and she always brought a boxful of things we couldn't buy: Marmite, self-raising flour, Cadbury's chocolate, bacon, condensed soup and lots of other goodies. We took the folk out and about and were always amused at their attitude to the weather. We had grown used to long, hot days but any time we were going out for the day, our friends would always grab a cardigan or a jacket. They found it hard to believe that one could be so sure that it wouldn't get cold, or rain!! They also insisted on opening the windows when it was hot and we would race around saying: "Shut the windows, please, you're letting the heat in!" Those poor, sun-deprived souls from Ireland couldn't get used to it at all!

At long last, it was time to catch the coach and head off for ten glorious days of holiday in Austria. The scenery was spectacular and we revelled in the amazing beauty of God's creation. The mountains were awe-inspiring and as we crawled round hairpin bends and zigzagged down steep slopes we just marvelled at the sheer wonder of what God had made. It was such a tonic and each day that passed we felt renewed and energised.

Back in Trévoux again we got an unexpected call from Martine. She wanted to arrange a meeting with us in Eddie's flat. Michel was invited too, as one of the leaders. We hoped this was a good sign. The day arrived and she cancelled! She told us she was getting married to David before the end of the year. We really felt she was courting disaster and we prayed desperately for her.

It would only be a couple of weeks before things started up again in Neuville. As we reflected on the past months they had been a real hotch-potch of experiences, some very good and some hard to swallow. We devoutly hoped that the second half of the year would be more settled and that our work in Neuville would make steady progress, but there was no guarantee of that happening.

September dawned and Eddie dropped his bombshell. He told us that he felt his time with Baptist Missions was coming to an end and he had informed them that he wanted to be free from the following September. We were totally unprepared for such news but he had obviously been thinking about it for some time and his mind was firmly made up. He had no intention of leaving France but planned to look for a secular job. That would mean the team would be down to just the two of us – we hardly dared think about that!

Since we met them in the market two years before, Florence and Michel, (mentioned in ch.3) had been coming to us more or less on a regular basis, but we could never depend on them being there. Michel had been a leader in the church that had split and we felt that he had been badly hurt and that was the reason he didn't want to become involved again. During the month of September we learnt that he had been going round to visit the folk in our group talking about the way we ran the various activities and saying that things were not going well. We didn't feel that was at all helpful and determined to sit down and have a good chat with him when we got the chance. The chance came a couple of weeks later. We talked quite openly with him and asked if he would come to us in future before going round the members. He agreed to that quite amicably but also said that we were going to have problems when we reached the point of actually constituting a church because there was a lot of anti-authority feeling around! This really depressed us and we began to wonder would we ever be able to feel that there was a church in Neuville strong enough to stand on its own feet, with godly, spiritual leaders who just wanted to serve the Lord.

A fortnight later Michel phoned us and asked if he and Florence could come and see us. They arrived looking very tense and tight-lipped. We had no idea why they had come but it was obviously something serious. Eventually we learned that he felt the problems they had had in their last church were going to happen once more and the pair of them had agreed they would rather leave than go through all that again. It appeared that their last pastor, an American, had been more of a dictator than a shepherd! We assured him that all decisions regarding the church that we formed would be taken by the French members, not by us, and if they didn't want a pastor, the church could function perfectly well under the guidance of elders. It would be up to the church to decide.

They stayed and talked until nearly midnight and we learnt a lot: of the need of French people to discuss at length every decision that would be taken (we had suspected that!); that our lack of fluency was not at all a problem (that was good to hear!), and that if their friend, Nicolas, Francoise's husband, came to church it would not be under duress but because he wanted to be there. All worth knowing. By the end of our chat we definitely knew each other a great deal better and we felt that if only they would stay with us and be committed, we'd find the work really going forward. Between them they had lots of gifts which would be invaluable in our little group.

We announced that a Ladies' Bible Study would start again on a Monday afternoon. I was quite looking forward to it. The three or four ladies who had come to it before had really enjoyed our time together and I hoped this session would be the same. I went down to the centre early, set out half a dozen chairs, and waited. And waited. The French are usually late. Wait a bit longer. But after half an hour, I knew nobody was coming, so I packed away the chairs and went home. Dear, oh dear!

Jean-Charles and Grazziella, the young couple converted in S.America, had been with us from the beginning. They had recently moved into one of the flats in our building in Trévoux. Just about this time they, too, seemed to have nothing but trouble. For a while Grazziella had been very depressed. We hadn't seen her at Neuville at all and we had the feeling she was hiding from us. Someone had smacked into their minibus and done considerable damage; their friend, Polo, was badly bitten by a dog while walking theirs; Jean-Charles lost his wallet with all his papers inside and a cupboard fell off the wall in their flat and smashed the WC!! What a catalogue of disasters! Through it all, Jean-Charles remained very faithful and one Sunday morning stood up and testified that God had given them victory over it all. The following Tuesday Grazziella appeared at the Bible Study, first time for ages. So at last we had something to really thank the Lord for!`

Our main encouragement came from our English classes. These were by no means 'direct evangelism' but they brought results, small but significant. Here are a few examples:

Eric, aged 28. Came to our church weekend. He said he was an atheist but had come willingly to two outreach events.

Annie, aged 50-plus. Came to an outreach film evening. Had never had a Bible and said she couldn't understand it anyway, but she bought a children's Bible and took it home to read.

Rémond, aged 70-plus. Became ill with cancer during the summer. We visited him and his wife and gave them a John's Gospel and prayed with them in their home. A few weeks later they came to the Sunday service to say thankyou for our prayers and to thank God that the latest tests for cancer were clear.

Xavier, aged 21. Had a Christian mother but told her he had no interest in spiritual things. At Hallowe'en he went to Ireland to spend two weeks with Christian families, to help his grasp of English.

These little events were such a blessing to us and showed us that our English Classes were really worthwhile, so it wasn't all doom and gloom.

New neighbours moved in beside us in Trévoux. They were English, much to my delight! Tony and Carole, with their two little girls had upped and left England because Tony felt France would be a much more moral country for his daughters to grow up in. Tony slept in our flat while waiting for his own goods and chattels to arrive with Carole and the children. Right from the start we got on really well together and were so pleased to have them living right beside us.

In October our friend, Tommy Lee arrived. He had been commissioned by the Mission to make a video of the work in Neuville. Having recently given up pig-farming in order to devote all his time to film-making, this was an important assignment for him. For ten days he followed us around and filmed everything we were doing, much to the amusement of the stall-holders in the market and the passers-by in the streets! Each evening we sat round and watched the day's 'shooting'. The interviews we did with some of our French friends were revealing: Marie-Annick, our downstairs neighbour showed a real interest in what we were doing and said she really enjoyed discussing things with us; Lynette's testimony was very humbling. She said she wanted to be like the team because we lived 'such upright lives'. That was a real challenge.

The only dissenting voice during the filming was that of Nicolas. For some reason he wasn't at all happy about it and said we hadn't given them enough warning. We often got the feeling that he really wasn't comfortable with us. Then the following Sunday when there were only five French adults present, Eddie was talking about the Huguenots and exhorting us to exhibit a like zeal. Afterwards Nicolas was really angry and said he was sick of being lectured, especially as his family was always there. True, but his attitude was incredible. The rest of our folk took the filming in their stride and even enjoyed being stars for the day.

The final product was called "Voilà Neuville" and was excellent. It would serve to give the people at home a real picture of what our life was like and would put faces to some of the names they had read in our Newsletters. That was all positive.

The year was coming to a close and we scheduled an Annual General Meeting for Nov. 26th. – and had to abandon it because only two ladies turned up! We re-scheduled it for later, and got on with giving out Bibles to some of our neighbours. Tony and Carole took one and said they'd be quite keen to send their little girls to Julie's Children's Club in the New Year.

At our General Meeting, in December, things were very positive. We had been expecting fireworks, but it wasn't too bad. Lynette talked a lot about wanting to be 'free' to go and find out about other groups and what they believed. We warned her of the dangers but agreed that she was free to do as she liked. Nicolas got up and announced that from that day on he no longer wanted to be an 'Active Member' and cheered up considerably having got that off his chest, insisting that they would continue to attend and give their money! Michel offered to help with the preaching and leading while we were in Ireland in January and February. Eight other folk chimed in with offers to help out and we felt it was really positive, for a change. We could leave for our time in Ireland knowing that things would continue without us and that the French folk were beginning to shoulder some responsibility. After such a year, that was distinctly hopeful!

Our last few days before leaving were marked by 8-10ins. of snow. The world looked really gorgeous and we thoroughly enjoyed being out in it. All our services had to be cancelled because nobody could get there so we had to leave without saying goodbye to our little flock. We knew Julie would keep us in touch with what happened while we were away. So off we went to Ireland for Christmas - and a £30 excess baggage charge at the airport!

Peter was planning his wedding: they'd opted for Eastertime. He was quite delighted to find that their first-choice hotel was fully booked up except for the day they had chosen. He thought that was amazing until I pointed out that their wedding day was to be Friday 13th!! No wonder it was free. What a good job all the other couples were superstitious!

7
HIGHS AND LOWS

The New Year started with a significant event in our life – we gained a lodger! Shirley was in France doing her 'year out' from University. She was about twenty and had been appointed to a teaching post in a huge 'lycée' in Lyon where her students were only a year or two younger than she was. With no teacher training behind her she felt she couldn't handle it and her classes were chaotic. To make matters worse she was staying with a French family where she wasn't happy. So the Lord sent her to us!

She arrived, mentally and emotionally exhausted and on the point of throwing up her University course altogether. We offered her our mezzanine as a safe haven and our sympathetic concern. Both of which she accepted gratefully. For a while she'd come in at the end of a long day and we'd hear her screaming to herself upstairs. Oh dear, another bad day! But gradually she regained her equilibrium and at least she felt she could let off steam with us, a thing she couldn't do with her French family. She bought herself a little 2-stroke motor-bike to get to and from Lyon, but without having much of a clue how to ride it, and would take herself off to explore the countryside. It wasn't too long before we got a phone call: "Come and rescue me – I'm in the ditch!!"

She livened up our lives immensely and we had many a good laugh together. We were delighted to see that she was coping much better with her classes and was much happier in herself. She learnt how to make bread-and-butter pudding and proudly served it up to us one evening; it was actually delicious! She proved to be a happy-go-lucky soul and when her term ended in June, our house seemed amazingly quiet.

On the church front, things were not going too well. Numbers on Sundays had fallen from about 30 to around 12-15; on Tuesdays only 4 or 5 turned up for the Bible Studies and the Youth work had closed because nobody came. 'Dear Lord,' we prayed. 'What on earth is going on? Things had looked so promising and now everything seems to be falling apart!'

Around this time, Corinthians became my preferred Daily Reading. How I could empathise with Paul as he struggled with a group of Christians who seemed to have little understanding of how to live for the Lord. We were in exactly the same position and his 'motto' became mine: WE DO NOT LOSE HEART! Over and over that little phrase appeared in my reading and it was a real blessing. The work in Neuville wasn't our work, it was God's and the outcome depended not on us but on Him. All we had to do was faithfully carry out the work He had given us to do. Hard-going it might be but every now and then a chink of light would glow in the darkness to remind us that God was still there and still working.

There weren't many bright spots in the first couple of months of 1990 but one of them was Florence, Nicolas' wife. She threw herself wholeheartedly into whatever was going on and really touched our hearts one day by asking George,"Would you prefer us to go somewhere else? There have been so many problems." We assured her we would much rather they stayed and really got stuck in!

One afternoon at the end of January, Lynette called in to the centre when George and I were 'on duty'. It was lovely to see her; she was a dear friend and our hearts had ached for her over the past year. George had made an appointment to go and have a chat with her the previous week and it seemed to have broken the ice. He determined to make appointments to go and visit all our folk one at a time to see if he could help with any problems. It seemed to bear fruit and little by little folk who had slipped away during the year began to filter back.

We had a surprise visit from Martine one day, up from the south to visit her relatives. She assured us she was fine and happy but we got the distinct impression that all was not well underneath. She skated over any personal questions and confined the conversation to generalities and we felt the smiles were a bit forced. Nevertheless she had renewed the contact and we could only commit her to the Lord.

In March and April we were in Ireland again. These yearly six-week tours seemed to come round amazingly often! This time we were looking forward to a very special day: Peter's wedding on the 13th. The day dawned, cold but sunny and the wedding was lovely, of course. Now we were 'in-laws' for the second time! After that really happy day, a week was all we had left before going back to Neuville.

George's mother wasn't at all well and had been in hospital all the time we had been home. The day before we were due to leave, we called up to the hospital to say goodbye to her. A nurse opened the main doors to us and asked who we wanted to see. George explained that we were leaving for France the next day and wanted to see his mother before we went. The nurse's face literally dropped and she looked very shocked. "Oh," she said.

"I'm so sorry. Your mother died early this morning and we've been trying to get in touch with you!" Poor George, the shock was tangible. He went in to see her for the last time and then we had the trauma of having to change all our travel arrangements so that we could go to the funeral. Because George was a pastor, the family always looked to him to take charge at times like this and he was asked to speak at the funeral. That was really hard for him but he did it and was able to say with confidence that he knew his mother had gone to be with the Lord.

Eventually we caught the plane and found ourselves back in Trévoux, after having had to pay £57 for 30kilos of excess baggage! We actually had 40kilos extra but the girl at the desk took pity on us!. News filtered through that the Youth Group had restarted and, thanks to a lot of publicity on Julie's part, they were getting quite a number of young people in. That was good to hear and we hoped it was perhaps a sign that things were picking up again.

We'd been back only a couple of weeks when we were invited to a meal at Julie's and Martine and her husband were going to be there, too. We had a nice, friendly time together and, just as we were preparing to leave, Martine asked if we would pray with them. We did so, and she sobbed all the way through it. Was she regretting all she had left behind? We didn't know, but something was happening in her heart. We didn't see her again that year at all and our hearts were sore for her. But she belonged to the Lord and we had to trust Him to look after her.

Tuesday nights continued with a faithful 4 or 5. There was a real sense of unity and everyone took part in the discussion and prayer-time. Florence remained loyal and faithful; she and her son, Emmanuel, never missed. Madame Bos, a retired lady who had recently come to us was also a regular attender. She regularly sent an advertisement of our weekly activities to a Lyon newspaper, and also played one hymn per week in our

Sunday services! Grazziella and Jean-Charles took it in turns to come and were visibly growing in their faith. We thanked God for these few and prayed that they would grow strong and stable.

In June, Eddie was making preparations to leave us. He had got a job teaching English in a school in Lyon and was very happy with that. One of his tasks during his time with us had been to look after our book-keeping, which he did with great efficiency. Now that he was going, the job fell to me and I really dreaded it. Years ago, when I was a student, I had looked after the accounts for the Christian Union, and at the end of each term when the books had to be handed in and checked, I was always kept until last because somehow mine never quite seemed to turn out right! So here I was, taking on that awful job again! We spent a whole afternoon together as Eddie sought to initiate me into the intricacies of the Association's books and I went home, books under my arm, and a sick feeling in my stomach. The Lord would really need to sharpen my brain to do this right.

With Eddie's departure looming, we were very pleased to learn that the Mission had agreed to appoint Julie as a full-time member of our team. She was very happy about it and so were we.

Early in June, we held our Church Weekend again. Last year we had been just a dozen; this year we were thirty-four! Everyone who could be there was there and there was a nice family atmosphere. Nicolas, Florence's husband, came and seemed at ease. He had started coming on Sunday mornings after several months' absence. Madame Bos brought two friends, retired ladies. They were very impressed by the friendliness shown to them and enjoyed the devotional times. Afterwards one of them confessed: 'I really enjoyed it, but you know I can't change my religion. I've always been a Catholic.'

We prayed that she would come to realise that what mattered most was to come to know God.

We expected things to be very quiet in July with most of our group away but in fact we had quite a busy month. We suspended the Bible Studies for the month and instead we tried something very new for us. We went out into the park or on to the riverside as a group, and sang! Now that may not seem at all extraordinary but in Neuville it was practically revolutionary! There were not many people around to hear us but that didn't matter. What counted was the enthusiasm of the folk who went out in fear and trembling and returned really thrilled to have attempted something new and different for the Lord. We were only half a dozen but they were so enthused that we went out and did it again a couple of weeks later!

On the two intervening Tuesdays, we 'borrowed' a Youth for Christ team from Ireland who were based for two weeks in Villefranche and they put on two 'Irish Nights' for us. These were very successful and each night there were over a dozen total outsiders in. What made it particularly rewarding for us was the fact that 6 or 7 of them were students from our English classes who had never before come to an evangelistic meeting. So all in all, July proved to be an encouraging month and the Lord put new heart into us.

At the end of August we had a farewell evening for Eddie and all the folk who he had known while in Neuville came into the centre to say goodbye to him. The friends had collected money for a gift for him and presented him with a really lovely camera. So another chapter closed. Eddie had been with us from the beginning and for him and for us it was a new era.

For our holiday, we spent ten very interesting days in Eastern Europe. The Berlin Wall had just come down a few months previously and we were amazed to see how quickly all signs of communism were being erased in Germany. We got our own personal chunk of the Wall and bore it home as a trophy! We spent a few days in Poland, and it was like stepping back into the 1940s. Nothing had progressed: we even saw a couple of folks out in the fields, the man ploughing with a horse and the woman following behind, sowing handfuls of seed from a basket. It was like a picture out of a children's Bible.

We paid an unforgettable visit to the camp at Auschwitz. That left indelible memories in our hearts. Everyone talked in whispers as we walked around, looking with horror at the huge glass cases filled with human hair, shoes of all shapes and sizes, and cases with their luggage labels still affixed. We walked through one of the buildings, the corridor lined with photos of those who had died there, and every so often a little bunch of flowers would be fastened under a picture of somebody's loved one. We actually stood in the gas chambers and saw the ovens, also strewn with flowers. People stood around with the tears flowing down their cheeks; it was a heart-rending experience. When we came outside again, the folk in our group wandered away to sit singly on benches in the grounds. The effect of that awful place made ordinary chat impossible.

We returned to Trévoux only to find a letter from my sister saying that her husband had died while we were away. He had had cancer for about five years . So it was a quick turn-around for me and a quick trip to Cornwall. It was inevitably a sad visit but it was good to see my mother and sister again.

The rest of the year passed quickly. Numbers gradually increased and we saw an increased willingness on the part of the French folk to shoulder responsibilities here and there. One encouraging activity was a 'Soirée Bible' which we held in November. Twenty-nine people came, of whom eight were 'outsiders'. We showed a video called 'the Book of Books'. The whole evening was conducted by French folk, the pastor from Villefranche gave a very good talk and we were able to just sit back and listen. Francoise and Michel had reappeared after several months' absence, and Michel led the whole evening.

Lynette, who had been away from the group for practically a whole year, started to come to services again and became an enthusiastic member of the Ladies' Bible Study group joining cheerfully in with the discussions and seeming very glad to be back with us.

So it was in a cheerful frame of mind that we prepared to leave Trévoux to spend Christmas in Ireland. Church Planting was proving to be a whole new experience for us. We'd lived through endless highs and lows but through it all we had seen God steadily and gently building His church in the midst of an area that had no knowledge of Him. That was thrilling.

We arrived back in the Emerald Isle just in time for the arrival of Grandson No.2 – Timothy Philip, born to Pauline and David on Christmas Eve. Another reason to celebrate. It was so good to see the family happy and well. It was especially good to see these little ones being added to the clan. We hoped there'd be plenty more!

8

Settling Down

The New Year had hardly started when news came from England; "Mum's had a stroke. Do you think you could come over?" That was a shock. We still had a couple of meetings to do before the end of our Deputation, but as soon as they were finished, I hopped on a plane and took the long journey to Cornwall. What would I find when I got there? I could never remember my mother as anything but fiercely independent and constantly on the go. How had this stroke affected her? I couldn't imagine how she would cope with being immobilised and I prayed that I wouldn't find her paralysed.

My sister met me at the bus-station and filled me in: Mother was in hospital, her speech was pretty bad but she didn't seem to be paralysed. I dreaded seeing her. After a cup of tea, we set out for the hospital. There was my Mum, in a large ward of about twenty beds. It was quite noisy and she, who fiercely guarded her independence, was now pretty much helpless and unable to communicate clearly. When she saw us, the tears started and I joined in! It was heart-rending, but after a few days I got more or less used to it and was able to spend a lot of time with her. She was 87 years old and had hardly ever been ill as far as I could recall so it was a huge shock to her system.

Eventually I had to leave, and that was hard but my sister promised to keep me informed and I knew she would do everything she could to make Mother's situation more bearable. Her faith in the Lord remained firmly fixed and we just had to trust her to His care.

As always, I wondered what we would find on our return to France. The last couple of years had been full of new experiences, a lot of them disappointing, and we had gone through hard times. Would this year be the same?

Amazingly, it proved to be wonderfully different! God was building His church and right from the start we saw the signs. There were a regular 20-30 folk at our Sunday service and about 12 at the Bible Studies. During the month a retired couple, M.and Mme Faure started to attend. They lived in Neuville and had heard about us from one of our ladies. They seemed thrilled at what they found in our little group and we hoped they would stay. The Lord was bringing us the ones and twos and our little family was growing.

Another new face was Chantal. She had come to know the Lord the previous summer at an open-air showing of the film 'Jesus' in Villefranche, but lived in Trévoux. In the same block of flats lived Josette, one of our 'regulars', who had invited her to join us in Neuville. She came to everything and soon began to talk about getting baptized.

We felt more encouraged than we had for a long time at this evidence that the Lord was with us and at work in our group. There was a feeling of expectancy in the air each time we met together and we even began to consider the possibility of officially constituting a church in the not-too-distant future.

Francoise and Michel, who had been with us on and off for a couple of years – and more off than on! - were proving to be very supportive. Francoise had taken charge of the Ladies' Bible Study while we were away, and she continued to do so. Lynette came to it regularly and started to attend on Sunday mornings again. Her husband remained more or less opposed to her association with us but she had learnt that she needed the support of other Christians and had a real desire to grow in her faith.

We started a Prayer Meeting on the last Thursday of every month just to pray for Neuville and each other. We started off with eleven people and it was really good to hear them praying for each other. There was evidence of a genuine bond being formed among us.

George went down with a bad dose of 'flu just about this time and couldn't seem to get back on his feet. He had constant headaches and just didn't feel well. He needed a break. The Lord already had things in hand! We heard that a good friend in Ireland had paid all the expenses for us to go to Spring Harvest, the big Christian festival, at Easter. That was wonderful news; we had heard a lot about it but had never been able to go before. Round about the same time, we were given a gift of money with specific instructions that it was to be used solely for indulging ourselves!! We deliberated for a while and finally decided to use it to buy a subscription to the local Gym and get ourselves fit. This we did and for a whole year we went faithfully twice a week to what the French call 'musculation'. We loved it and it certainly helped George to get over his bad patch. Once again we had been reminded of the privilege of belonging to the family of God, and the generosity of its members.

On the last Sunday in March we had 31 at our service which turned out to be a bit chaotic. The clocks had gone forward the night before. Florence was supposed to be leading the service and some of her children were to do the readings. They didn't turn up – they had forgotten to change their clock!! In the end we started without them, frantically choosing hymns as we went along. Half an hour later, in they all came, very flustered – to the knowing grins of the rest of the congregation! A lady called Marie had been asked to sing. She had no music and halfway through she forgot the words and sat down in confusion, to sympathetic murmurs from the folk around her. A black couple were there for the first time and he asked if he could sing! We didn't know them at all, but thought we would risk it! Fortunately it turned out well and he just sang a nice little chorus. That was a relief. Another couple arrived an hour late. The girl stood up and testified that since the monthly prayer meeting, she had been sleeping soundly, a thing she hadn't been able to do for months! So, in spite of it all, we had a really good morning. We loved the informality of our gatherings and the willingness of our people to share what was going on in their lives. We felt that was a really healthy sign of trust among us.

In April I received my first 'outside' speaking engagement. We had friends in Lyon, John and Sue Smith, who were working with the English Baptist Union. It was Sue who invited me to her house group. I spent a few hours preparing and just a couple of days before the meeting I developed a roaring sore throat. I knew what that meant: the next day or two I'd be spluttering and coughing with a streaming cold! And, true to form, that's what happened. I could hardly see out of my eyes and got through hundreds of tissues! My voice began to go, too, so I was in fine form as I set off to drive to Lyon! There were nine ladies present and as I struggled through my talk on 'Our walk with the Lord', I sensed that they were really listening intently. The Lord gave me the strength to get through it and I was really encouraged by the discussion that followed. I'd taken a few books with me from our shop and these were seized upon eagerly and quite a few were bought. Sue was so pleased with the ladies' reaction and felt it had been a very worthwhile evening. I felt like a wet rag afterwards and was exhausted by the time I had driven back to Trévoux, but what a blessing it was to be able to teach folk about the Lord and to see genuine interest in spiritual things. It had done me the world of good.

Two of my most faithful English class students suddenly turned up at our Sunday morning services. They were Rémond, who'd had cancer, and Annie, a lady in her fifties. Neither of them had any experience of church life and Annie especially found it a whole new world. She came in one Sunday having just done her morning shopping, basket in one hand and two baguettes under her arm. She marched up to the front row, propped her baguettes against the wall and while we were waiting for others to arrive, she took her newspaper out of her basket, opened it up and in a loud voice began Oh-la-la-ing about the items of news that she read! So I had to quietly explain to her that it might be a good idea to save the news until she got home!

Our friendship with the German family who lived beside us was flourishing. Matthias' parents came over from Frankfurt for two weeks and we were invited over to the flat for a meal with them. They were a delightful couple. She came from a Catholic background and he was a Protestant and it wasn't long before the conversation seemed to turn quite naturally to salvation by faith and they discussed with us for ages while Katarina and Matthias just listened. It was really good and we were thrilled to see Katarina and her mother-in-law at our Bible Study on the following Tuesday night. It was based on Luke 15 and a lovely opportunity to look at God's love for us. They both seemed to enjoy being there: the seed was sown.

We planned a baptismal service for May and Chantal started to come to George for preparation classes. Florence's young daughter, Sophie came too . She was only about ten years old but George found her really clear about what she was doing and Florence had spent time explaining things to her.

The day of the baptism dawned, and for the first time it was Michel who did the baptising. Forty-five people were present, including Rémond and Annie to whom the whole service was something quite new. After a happy morning together we went back to Trévoux to discover that Katarina and Carole, our friends, had organised a barbecue in the garden. They had gathered up everyone from our building and were just waiting for us to come home from church. We all stayed outside for the whole afternoon and it was lovely to have all the neighbours together talking and playing 'Boules' and enjoying each others' company. It's a rare thing in France, and we felt that it was maybe the outcome of having all us 'foreigners' in the building. Whatever the reason, it was good to belong to this little community whom we regarded in many ways as our private 'mission field'. Marie-Annick told us that they were having a new house built at the top of the road and so would be moving out of the flat below us as soon as their new home was finished. That was a blow; we had become firm friends over the years but at least they wouldn't be too far away and we would still be able to see them.

At the end of May, Julie told us that 'someone' was prepared to pay for Fiona to come over for a visit. We had no idea who this kind benefactor was, but we praised God for them. We phoned Fiona and told her and she was very excited. We were due to go up to Paris in June for a Field Council with our fellow missionaries up there, so asked Fiona to arrange her flight so that we could meet her while we were there. She duly arrived, thrilled to be back in the hot sunshine – and to see us, of course! We had a happy two weeks together, exploring new places and hearing all the news from home.

While she was over, the time came round for our annual Church Weekend and she came with us. We were a group of 49 this year, 13 of whom were not Christians. Chantal's husband came, and she told us later that, when they returned home, for the very first time she was able to talk to him seriously about her faith. Several of our students came; Annie brought her husband, a lovely quiet man who fitted in well, Rémond came and a young man called Xavier. We began to see the value of our English classes more and more.

The month of June also saw the signing, after two years of waiting, of the papers making the centre in Neuville the property of Irish Baptist Missions. So it was now ours and in that sense the future of our little church was secure. That was a huge step forward.

In July, Julie organised a fête for the Children's Club: races, team games, food etc. Florence said they could have the eats at her house afterwards. She lived in a little village in the hills above Neuville where there was plenty of grass for the games. At the very last minute, Florence suddenly announced that none of her children would be going, they'd had enough fêtes, and they couldn't use her house either! This was all very upsetting and we did wonder if Nicolas had been unhappy with the arrangements but we didn't know that for sure. In the end, only three children turned up. It was all a big disappointment and quite hurtful, all the more so when it came from Florence who had been so faithful all along.

Francoise and Michel organised a meal in their garden for everyone in our group, to celebrate Chantal's baptism, before we all left for the summer holidays. It was very hot, and we were grateful for the shade of the trees. There was quite a crowd of us. We ate a lovely meal together and then sang for an hour. It was so nice to see how well our little church family got on together. At the end of the afternoon, Chantal stood up and prayed, thanking God for all His blessings. Her husband and children were there, and it took courage to stand up and be counted but Chantal told us afterwards that Serge, her husband, had commented on the fact that we all seemed so happy together. It had really impressed him.

Just before things closed down for the summer, I asked Annie if she would like us to read the Bible together and she said she would, so we arranged to set a time to do that after the holidays. Another step forward!

In August we went back to Ireland to work on refurbishing a small house we had bought in Belfast. It had been fairly cheap, but was in a dreadful state of repair and we wanted to do some basic DIY so that Fiona could move into it. She had been living in a rather unsavoury area of Belfast and we wanted her to be somewhere safe. She had horrified us once by telling us that she had arrived home late one night to find a drunk man lying across her garden path! That added a sense of urgency to the repairs and, happily, by the end of the month she was finally installed. She was delighted to be in her own house and not some dingy rented property, and we knew she would take good care of it. We left to go back to France, feeling much happier about her situation.

September brought everybody back from their holidays and also brought us significant help. Samuel and Raija arrived in Neuville. He was French and she was from Finland. They were full-time workers with Youth for Christ and we were thrilled to welcome them. They were a lovely young couple who knew what the Christian life was all about, and we knew that they would bring a real stability to our folk. Samuel quickly got involved with the Youth Group and Julie was able to take a few of them for a weekend to the Youth for Christ centre.

Once again attendances were good from the word go, and we really began to feel that the work in Neuville had turned the corner. Francoise offered to do the window display on alternate months. She was very artistic and we knew she would bring real flair to the job. Florence announced that she intended to start a Good News Club in her home, (no explanation of what had happened over the fête!). Julie said she would help her and would bring a couple of children from Neuville with her. They duly started, but the results were disappointing. Some days nobody turned up and only one child from the immediate area came to the Club. Florence refused to be discouraged and went to the mayor to ask permission to advertise the Club in the local press.

And then I started to have Bible Studies with Annie, which proved to be very interesting. She had never in her life read the Bible and had absolutely no idea what it was all about. We started with the Gospel of John because I thought that would be a good place to start. But, oh dear, try explaining the first chapter to someone without any knowledge of the Bible! Over the weeks we persevered and sometimes I would feel we were really getting somewhere and then she would ask a question that showed that we weren't! One day we were talking about the Holy Spirit and she exclaimed, "Fancy that! I never knew that the Holy Spirit had anything to do with God!" Another time, in the course of discussion, I discovered that she had never heard the Christmas story. It was hard to credit, but I promised we would read it the next week.

During September we did another leaflet drop. It was a long time since we had made a concerted effort to reach the homes in the town, and this time we gave out 2500 leaflets, introducing ourselves and saying what we stood for. It took hours of walking to cover the whole town and it all had no visible effect whatsoever! We did wonder if perhaps that sort of distribution was really of any value. It took up such a lot of our time and didn't seem to achieve anything much.

October saw us concentrating on Outreach and trying to encourage our folk to get involved. We held a 'Friendship Evening' in the centre in Neuville and asked our folk to make a real effort to bring along a relative or friend who so far had never been to any of our activities. It was very successful in that we welcomed 25 people on the night. Our members had prepared a very nice meal and at the end of the evening, Francoise stood up and spoke very sincerely about her faith and she was given close attention by all the visitors. So with that success in mind, we invited our folk to think about doing the same thing in their own homes. But, from what we could glean, we seemed to be the only ones who were planning to do so.

I organised a special Ladies Evening in our flat and invited every lady in the building to come along. I asked the wife of the Villefranche pastor to come and talk about Christmas. She was a very talented lady and had already published a book about how Christmas was celebrated across the world. She also had a beautiful collection of Nativity scenes from various countries and I asked her to bring them with her for the ladies to see. Some of the Polish ones were amazing works of art, composed of little bits of shiny paper and odds and ends. I made a quick dash to Lyon for an M&S Christmas cake for the evening, and all was set. It all went very well. The Christmas Story was recounted in all its lovely simplicity, the ladies learnt how to make a pretty decoration for their tables and they admired the Nativity scenes. We sat and talked afterwards for ages and they left having enjoyed their evening.

Just a couple of days before Christmas we were in our flat when the phone rang. George lifted it and a little voice the other end said: "Hullo, Grandad. Listen…." And wee Mark sang 'Away in a Manger' all the way through! What a lovely Christmas greeting! I have to admit that for me the tears weren't far away. It made me feel, very acutely, the pain of separation, missing all those lovely baby-days, first words, first funny little sayings etc.

Financially, December had been a very difficult month. For some unknown reason the money that came into the bank for us was much less than usual and we had presents to buy and food for entertaining as well as all the usual bills to pay and it just wasn't enough. And once again we saw God at work providing for all our needs: for the first time ever since being in France, we received money gifts in some of our Christmas cards. That had never happened before, and we were so grateful.

Christmas day we spent on our own,- for the first time ever, just the two of us. It seemed very strange, but we ate turkey with all the trimmings and opened our presents and did all the usual things. It was awfully quiet! In the evening we went down to Lyon and joined John and Sue Wilson and family for fun and games. They had several young people over from England as well and we had a riotous evening. It was great fun, and finished the day off nicely for us.

On Boxing Day we invited Carole and Tony and children, with Katarina and Matthias and their family to come in. They arrived about 3pm and we had a hilarious afternoon being entertained by Tony with his box of magic tricks. The children certainly enjoyed the fun and then we adults played "PIT" which brings out the real competitive spirit and those who like to cheat can have a field day! It was noisy and tiring and very relaxing. They all stayed until about 9o'clock, by which time all the children were dropping with sleep. Goodnights were said and off they trooped to their respective flats. We cleared up the room and fell into our armchairs, tired but happy. How blessed we felt to have made such good friends here! We loved them all but our dearest wish was to see them coming to know God for themselves. Until that day we would cherish our friendship with them and keep them in our prayers.

We were trying 'by all means to save some.' Some efforts were outwardly more successful than others but all were worth trying. Our aim was to honour the Lord in all these things and to use any means at our disposal to bring them to Him. Somebody once said; "What we're doing is building bridges into people's lives so that one day the Lord Jesus can walk across." I thought that was lovely and that was exactly what we were trying to do in the Saône Valley.

Joshua 13 v.1 says, "There are still very large areas of land to be taken over." How true that was for us! As we looked at France and the enormous need of the French people who, in general, lived lives totally unaware of God or of His love for them, it was enough to make the bravest heart quail. But God said to Joshua:"Be strong and courageous." And He was saying the same to us and above all we knew that He would be with us whatever happened and with the embryo church in Neuville.

So ended another year. It had on the whole been a year of progress and encouragement. The church was slowly forming and the Christians were learning about their faith, some quicker than others but all bound together by our Christian family ties. It was good and we were much more encouraged than we had been for a long time. God was at work, and we had seen evidence of it all around us.

9
Disappointments And Encouragements

February '92 saw us glued to our television whenever we had a moment in order to watch the Olympic Games. An abiding memory from that time was watching the bobsleigh rides. At the side of the track somebody kept flipping up a placard with 'John 3:16' printed on it in big letters. The French commentator obviously hadn't the faintest idea of the significance of the reference and he commented: "There's a certain 'John' here who seems to have lots of support!!" Amusing but oh, so revealing.

The same lack of familiarity with the Bible was shown in our church one day. Julie had given a little girl a Bible verse to read out. This she did, very nicely and then she came to the reference at the end which was John 7:9-14. She announced: "John 7 divided by nine minus 14!!" Things which we took so much for granted were totally foreign to most of the French folk we were dealing with, and sometimes we tended to forget that.

I continued to meet with Annie once a week for Bible Study. We were progressing slowly through John's Gospel and arrived at the story of the woman caught in adultery. We read the story and then I asked her: "Why do you think Jesus didn't condemn her?" Annie pondered for a moment and then replied:"Perhaps He knew He'd done something just as bad!!" And that, after weeks of trying to explain that Jesus was God's Son, perfect and holy. Sometimes I despaired of ever making any progress with her but it reinforced to me what I already knew very well i.e. that if the Holy Spirit didn't open her understanding, she would never make sense of what we were reading. When we reached the story of the Crucifixion, she asked, "Did the two thieves come back to life, too?"

A few weeks later, we were at home in our flat when the phone rang. It was a young man who introduced himself as Pierre. He had met our son Peter at a YMCA conference in Denmark, and said he had a 'pacquet' (package) for us, and was just checking that we would be at home if he brought it. We assured him we would and then waited in anticipation for him to arrive. What on earth could Peter be sending us?

Half an hour later, the doorbell rang, and Pierre presented the 'pacquet'- nothing less than Peter himself! After Denmark they had attended a YMCA Week in France and this was the last day before going back home. What a thrill it was to see him! I could hardly believe my eyes, and, idiotically, the first thing I blurted out was, "What on earth are you doing here?" We were able to spend practically the whole day together and it was better than a tonic!

Just about this time our little Opel Kadett belched out smoke and died. At least it seemed to us to be dead, but our neighbour, Tony, spent hours with George, taking out all the bits and pronounced it curable. Whatever it needed, it was going to cost quite a bit and we had no extra cash to spare. I said to the Lord, 'You know how much this is going to cost and You are wholly aware of our money situation. Please work it out!' Tony brought back a few parts from England and left George a list of instructions. From then on the rain poured down ceaselessly; the car was up on a pile of bricks, Tony was on a trip to Russia, and nothing could get done. Julie was in Ireland, doing her tour of the churches and she had left her car, saying we could use it if we needed to; so that was a temporary solution to the problem. While we waited, we spent a weekend with my long-lost cousin in Grenoble. As we were leaving he gave George an envelope with strict instructions not to open it until we got home.

When we got back, we saw Tony's car parked in the drive. Good, he was home! So before we even went inside our own door, George went round to ask Tony his assessment of the damage. He estimated the cost at round about £300. Our hearts sank to our boots. That was a lot! Help! Once inside our flat, George remembered the envelope we'd been given. He opened it and inside was….You've guessed it - £300!! God never ceased to amaze us.

Margaret, our ex-colleague, and her husband, Robert, came to spend a weekend with us. They brought with them a video entitled, 'From Despair to Hope', the stories of Van Gogh and Rembrandt and their search for God. They recommended it highly and I thought I might invite one or two of the neighbours to come in and watch it. In the end, about six folk came, including Katarina and Marie-Annick from our building, Annie and Francoise from Neuville and a couple of their friends. I felt that the video was a bit 'preachy' but the ladies all seemed to be really interested in the story and sat discussing for ages afterwards. Our desire was for them to realise they needed to know God for themselves, rather than finding salvation just an interesting topic for debate! Patience …..patience.

Our 'council' or oversight at Neuville consisted of George and I, Julie, Samuel the Youth for Christ worker, Michel and Florence. We were so pleased to find that from the beginning of the year there was a very positive attitude in all our meetings, not a sign of tension anywhere and a genuine desire on the part of everyone to see the work in Neuville moving forwards. Francoise continued to do the window-dressing on alternate months and produced some really eye-catching displays. She did it cheerfully and well and seemed to really enjoy it. Her husband, Michel, was taking an increasing share of the preaching and it was improving markedly; there was far less philosophy and much more Biblically-based teaching and we rejoiced to see it.

Florence at last received a reply from the mayor re advertising her Good News Club in the village press. It was to be advertised as a 'Protestant Catechism'. We were a bit taken aback by that because we felt it would immediately preclude any contact with the Catholic families in the village, but 'God meant it for good'. As a result of the advert, she and Julie were invited to talk about their faith with a group of about twenty teenagers who asked really searching questions and wanted to know the meaning of 'conversion' etc. So that was an excellent outcome.

Our friendship with our neighbours was growing and one evening we were invited, along with Carole and Tony, to a meal in Katarina's flat. We had a super meal and then sat around the table talking until it was time for the children to go to bed. Once they were safely tucked up, the real discussion of the evening began and it wasn't long until the conversation turned to our church-planting activities. It gradually became more personal and soon we were talking about conversion and baptism. The chat went on until about 2am when we all decided it was about time we went to bed. We felt so glad that we were able to have such discussions with our friends but as yet the light didn't seem to be dawning.

Family news was good: two more grandchildren expected later in the year – Pauline and David's third, and Peter and Pauline's first! When we consulted the calendar we were delighted to discover that we would be back in Ireland at least for the arrival of the first one. News about Mother was mixed. She had been moved from the hospital because it was closing down and all the NHS patients had been transferred to a rather palatial nursing home at the other side of the town. That was an answer to prayer: neither my sister nor I could have afforded the exhorbitant fees demanded, but mother was there with no cost at all. That was wonderful, but she had lately developed an ulcer on her leg that was proving difficult to heal. She had just started to walk, albeit slowly, with a walking aid, but now was confined to her room again. My sister reported that mother was in good spirits and was being well looked-after. It was just a matter of waiting for things to improve.

Back in Ireland for a few weeks, we were thrilled to welcome grandson No.3 to the world. Michael Scott was born on June 9th, weighing in at 9lbs. He was a bonny, bouncing baby and we were very happy to share in the first few weeks of his life. Our reception by the churches was as warm and caring as usual and we were able to meet up with lots of folk who assured us that they prayed for us every day. I always found that amazing – and very humbling, and we were so grateful to know we had such constant support.

We returned in time for our next Summer Team from Ireland. As usual there was a good response to all the planned activities, with our English class students turning up to nearly everything. Rémond, the 70-yr old, took a copy of Ultimate Questions and went away to read it. Annie came to a Tuesday Bible Study for the very first time and with these small steps forward we felt encouraged. The team members were all invited out to meals with our church folk and that was a great success and cemented Franco-Irish relationships in a way nothing else could have done. One of us went with each group to do any necessary interpreting and it was great.

It was especially good for Julie. She accompanied three or four folk to a home in Lyon and found that there was an extra guest invited, besides the team. He was a young English fellow, working as an engineer in Lyon and a work-colleague of the girl whose house they were in. His name was Lionel and we discovered later that he had been very attracted to Julie and that the two of them had met up again during the summer break and things were moving fast. That was a development we hadn't anticipated!

In August, the centre in Neuville closed down for the holidays and we prepared to go off to Germany for three weeks. We were really looking forward to it, not just because we would be in a new country, but because we had been invited by Katarina and Matthias' parents to stay with them. We were excited at the chance of getting to know them better and asked the Lord to give us opportunities to speak to them about Him.

As it turned out, we had an excellent three weeks. They were so kind, and went out of their way to give us a good time. We were taken on a trip down the Rhône where we were able to see all the fairytale castles along the riverside. We visited the German Parliament buildings which were very impressive. The weather was lovely and we walked a lot and altogether really enjoyed the break. We spent two weeks with Matthias' parents and on the last morning, Anne-Marie, his mother, asked if she could share my daily Bible reading with me. I agreed very happily and we sat in the garden and read and discussed and prayed and she said she felt it had really helped her.   Leaving them, we travelled over to stay with Katarina's mother, a widow. She lived in a charming bungalow surrounded by a real old-fashioned cottage garden, obviously her passion. This week wasn't quite so easy-going because our hostess didn't speak any English or French!! That presented quite a problem but sign language can achieve quite a lot, and I dredged up my school German from thirty years before and managed to make myself understood, more or less. We were in a really olde-worlde village with cobbled streets and a witch's tower! The houses were bedecked with flowers and it was all a bit 'Brothers Grimm'. We loved it and explored every corner.

Too soon, much too soon, the holidays were over and it was back to Neuville. After five years of 'sowing' we very much wanted to start reaping a harvest, but that was God's prerogative: we just needed to keep plodding on, working with the folk God had given to us and helping them to grow in their faith.

In October we took the decision to change the name above our premises to 'Eglise Protestante Evangelique'. We had the right to do that even though we weren't yet formally constituted as a church. We felt it was time for the town to appreciate that we were more than just a French-Irish Association. As a direct result of seeing the sign several people came in to ask about what we were doing, so it did have an impact.

Hospitality-wise, we had a very busy month. George and I made out a list of all the contacts we had made over the years in Trevoux and we invited them for meals. In all we had 15 folk in, in ones and twos. They were all unconverted, non-church-going folk and we knew that for most of them the only Christian input into their lives came from us. That was such a responsibility! As a general rule, the French are not renowned for their friendliness, particularly to foreigners, but we had proved that perseverance paid off and had made lots of good relationships with folk we had met. These were precious people and we coveted them for the Lord.

At the end of November, if I'd been asked to name the qualities necessary to be a missionary in France, I would have to have added a new one: a thick skin! Julie and I decided to try a new venture one afternoon. In our area at that time of the year, it was common practice for the firemen, the postmen, the societies for the blind etc. to go from door to door selling calendars. Normally we avoided knocking on people's doors, but we thought we would try selling Scripture calendars in Neuville. Not wanting to waste our funds, we bought just thirty calendars with a tear-off Bible verse for each day.

We set out, hearts high with expectation. After all, we had prayed a lot about this new effort; maybe the Lord would really use us and in a couple of days we might have them all sold. It was a beautiful afternoon,- bright blue sky, leaves glowing with autumn colours. 'God's in His heaven, all's right with the world', and off we went.

Julie took one side of the road and I took the other. We were in a well-to-do part of the town, nice houses, big gates. The first house, lady in the garage, working. I opened the gate and walked in.

"Bonjour, Madame! I'm from the Protestant church here in Neuville and I have Scripture Calendars for sale."

"I don't want one. Take it away!"

"Could I just leave you an invitation to our special events this month?"

"No, you couldn't. I'm not interested."

Dear me, what a start! No 'goodbye', no smile, no nothing. I continued up the road. A lot of the gates were locked and I couldn't get in, so I left an invitation in each mail-box.

I saw a man sweeping up the leaves.

"Bonjour, Monsieur. Would you like to buy a Scripture calendar?"

"No, I wouldn't. It doesn't interest me."

"Well perhaps you'll accept this invitation…" He took it, scanned it quickly and handed it back.

"No. I don't want it. Goodbye."

And so it went on. A fierce Alsatian barked on top of the next wall. There was no way I was going to put anything in that mailbox! We persevered, but at house after house we got a refusal in varying degrees of abruptness.

Next house. The name on the gate was Mr. Nightingale. I called across to Julie: "At least these should be pleasant!" They were. I explained who I was and Mr. Nightingale informed me that his wife sold calendars for the Catholic Church! He didn't seem to be too sure what to do with me so he called his wife. Seeing the address on the invitation she said: "Oh, you're the people in Rue Victor Hugo. Your group is very active, isn't it?" My flagging spirits lifted. At least someone in Neuville had heard of us. She took the invitation but refused a calendar and said goodbye.

How was Julie faring? At the end of the first street she had managed to sell a calendar to a little old man who spoke courteously to her. Our hearts took courage but after that, at house after house she was turned away. Opening a gate, she went up the steps and knocked. Hearing somebody call "Entrez!", she opened the front door and stepped inside, only to be met a moment later by an indignant householder. Retreating rapidly, Julie tried to explain: "I'm sure I heard someone say 'Come in'…" Sad to say, she was very much mistaken and the irate lady did not buy a calendar!!

A few refusals later, Julie arrived at the last house on her side. She was still a bit shaky from the previous faux-pas but she opened the gate, walked up the steps to the door, and knocked.

A window opened upstairs and a lady shouted down to ask her business. Julie explained, only to be met with: "You've got a nerve, coming up to the door! Why didn't you ring the bell at the gate and wait outside?" Was there any point in explaining that she hadn't noticed the bell?

We met at the end of the street. We'd been out for nearly two hours and in unison we declared that we'd had enough. What an afternoon! Our spirits were bruised and battered and what had we accomplished? We tried mutual encouragement: "Don't let's get depressed. The sky is just as blue now as when we started! The Lord knows all about it, and the outcome is up to Him".   At least there was one nice little man with 365 Bible verses in his home. God bless him!

Humanly speaking, it had been a bad afternoon and, as was the case so often in France, our efforts for the Lord seemed to fall on stony ground. But we had had to learn not to worry about the results – they belonged to God. So home we went, trying hard not to feel downhearted. At least we had tried! A couple of weeks later I tried the same thing in Trévoux, but although the reception was kinder, nobody wanted to buy.

In that same month we had three film evenings in the centre. The first film was 'Joni'. Thirty people came in, of whom twelve were complete strangers. We were a bit disappointed that not one of the folk we personally had invited, came, but what was encouraging was that all the strangers had been invited by our church members. That was a new thing and we thanked God for it. The second film was mainly for young people and there were nineteen at it, mostly from our own circle, and the third was on the subject of Incarnation and several folk had promised to come. On the night there was quite a crowd and Katarina was among them. They watched the film with rapt attention and the question time was lively. The young man who presented the evening was very adept at answering even the most tricky queries and he presented the Bible truth clearly and well. All in all, a success.

In December, Julie announced that she and Lionel had provisionally set a wedding date for April 24th of the following year. They hoped to meet each other's parents at Christmas and if all went well, would get officially engaged after that. Exciting news, especially as they stressed the fact that although Julie would be leaving the Mission team, she and Lionel would continue to be members of the Neuville church – and they wanted George to conduct the wedding ceremony!

I was still going to Annie's home each week to read the Bible. We had finished the Gospel of John and had commenced some of the Old Testament stories. All seemed to be going well and then, out of the blue, we got a letter saying that she wouldn't be coming to anything more in the centre and didn't want me to go to her house again! Totally inexplicable, but there was nothing we could do but respect her wishes, and wait. It was all very strange.

Just before leaving to go to Ireland for Christmas, we held our Field Conference in Paris. The Mission Secretary was present and, half joking, he asked if I'd like to go to Peru to teach the missionary children while their teacher was doing language study. It started off as not really serious, but the more we talked, the more it felt right. I had trained as a Primary teacher, and it was something I loved doing. He agreed that George could go too, and that was a blessing because he really needed a break. It was an opportunity that would never come again! Originally, the plan was that we would go for August, September and October but then it was decided that if we went in July, we could join a group that was going out from Ireland to visit all the different areas of our missionaries' work and we could see it for ourselves. We said we would give a final decision in a week's time. But I think in our hearts we both knew that we would do it. Another adventure looming!!

With that exciting prospect finalised, we approached another family Christmas. Little Megan Fiona, our first granddaughter, had arrived safely in September, so we were looking forward to making her acquaintance, and of course to see the rest of our ever-increasing family. We packed our bags, said goodbye to our French 'family' and set off for the airport en route to Ireland once more.

10

Reaching Out

1993 started off painfully; we got our first set of vaccinations for going to Peru. We both had nasty reactions, feeling shivery and sore and my arm swelled up and was hot and angry for days, but at least we should be protected from cholera, typhoid and yellow fever! It was confirmed by the Mission that we would be in Peru from July to November. Including our two months of Deputation, that meant that our little church in Neuville would be without us for six months of the year. We felt that this might prove to be a good thing for the church, as the folk would have to take responsibility for everything themselves

We were in Ireland for Deputation during January and February and after one meeting the pastor's wife invited us back for supper. After coffee and the inevitable cream-with-everything eats, she asked if we'd be interested in some second-hand clothes. Being always open to offers, we said yes and for the first time we experienced the joys of the 'Missionary Barrel'. The clothes were all in very good condition and George ended up with two nearly-new suits and three pairs of trousers. I got a lovely red jacket (which I'm still wearing 14 years later!), a skirt, culottes and a couple of jumpers. We were really pleased with it all and very grateful to the unknown donors.

We returned to France at the end of February and a couple of weeks later, Fred McCurry, one of the joiners who had helped us so much in the past, came out again. This time he was going to remove a wall in our Centre and replace it with moveable pine panels so enabling us to enlarge our church space. We were expecting a team of thirty-five young people for a week's evangelism at Easter and we definitely needed more room. Fred was a big, quiet man who loved the Lord and gave his time and his skills very willingly in the service of our little church. We loved having him with us and really enjoyed his company.

Just before Christmas we had received a mysterious note from Annie saying she wouldn't be coming to us any more, but on our return from Ireland she contacted us and said she'd had a knee operation but would be back when she was better. We found this sort of thing inexplicable. Strange things happened and we never seemed to be given any explanation for them. We just had to live with it. So at the end of February I turned up at her home again and we continued our Bible Studies. We began to look at a little book entitled 'Assurance en Christ' which explained clearly about salvation. I prayed that this would help her to understand the Gospel which was all so new to her.

France's evangelical churches were preparing for a series of Billy Graham relays from Essen in Germany which would be seen in several centres across the country in March. The Lyon newspaper, 'Le Progres', published an excellent article on Billy Graham showing pictures of him in action, and describing him;

"unlike other television evangelists he remains a preacher above all suspicion". It reported that there were 170 sites across the region ready to receive this 'Grand Show Televisé'. It was really encouraging to read such an unbiased and sympathetic write-up. The evangelical church in France was so small, one group for every 250,000 of population, and generally overlooked or unknown, so this publicity was a real boost for little struggling churches.

We began to ask our friends and neighbours if they would come with us to the Relays. Annie promised to come and so did Xavier so that was a start. George, Julie and I arranged to meet in our centre in Neuville from 1.30-2.00pm every day from the beginning of March to pray for the campaign and we invited our church people to come and join with us. It was disappointing that only two of them came: Samuel, the Youth for Christ worker and Francoise. There seemed to be little interest in such an important event with such potential, but we had found over the years that the French folk had little appetite for evangelism. We had mentioned the campaign to all the neighbours in our building and to all our English students. Nobody refused but there was no knowing who would actually come. We prayed that the Lord would bring along the folk that He wanted to be there.

The first evening of the Relays was for Christians and we were happy to see seven of our church folk present. The challenge was there to use this opportunity to reach out to others and to rededicate our lives to the Lord's service. The next night the outreach began in earnest. Xavier came with us and drank in the message, At the end he said he didn't go forward because it would have been dishonest; he wasn't ready to do it. We appreciated his honesty and felt that he had been challenged by what he had heard. During the rest of the week we saw several of our invitations being taken up; Marie-Annick and Gilles both came; Rémond was there and brought his wife, and Annie came too. And so the week passed.

On the last night, Mme.Ponsot came with us. She was a little lady in her 70's who lived near us. I had been spending an hour every week with her for the past couple of years, principally for her to practise her English. She was a very artistic person and painted on silk and porcelain, delicate little designs of leaves and flowers. She was also an avid bird-lover, an interest I shared, and we would sit for ages watching the activities of the birds on her balcony where she laid out margarine tubs of seeds and nuts to attract them. We had begun to talk about faith and belief in God and she had shown me a much-treasured Bible which had belonged to her mother. It had obviously been well-read with various verses underlined. It was evident that this Book had been important in her mother's life and that opened the door to many a good discussion. So I was very glad to see her at the Relays and although she didn't show any signs of having been touched by what she heard, the message had been faithfully proclaimed and we had to trust that the Holy Spirit would open her heart to receive it.

The following Sunday we invited Xavier to lunch, along with a newly-converted young man called Philippe who had recently joined us in Neuville. The two of them really hit it off well, and we were delighted to hear them planning to go jogging together. Philippe was very enthusiastic about his new-found faith and he talked for ages with us about his Christian life and what it meant. Xavier just sat and took it all in and before leaving said, "I might come down to Neuville with you next Sunday." He had never come to church with us even though he had come to lots of other activities, so we were thrilled. The French have a saying: 'Little by little the bird builds her nest', and that's how we felt about our work for the Lord in France. Little signs of growth, little steps in understanding, little glimmers of light dawning in someone's life; these were the things that kept us going when outwardly there was not much to encourage.

A young widow, a friend of Julie's, had been converted through the Billy Graham Relays and her life had really been transformed. She had never read the Bible and we were amazed at how quickly she learned spiritual truths in the subsequent weeks. Her growth in the Lord was evident to everyone and she never missed any of our meetings in Neuville. We praised God for her and were glad to have her with us. Like many of the French folk we met, her life was a mess; family-wise, work-wise and in practically every other way she seemed to have amassed enormous problems. The future was going to be hard for her and we prayed that the Lord would keep her close to Himself.

Mid-April saw the arrival of our team of young people from Ballynahinch and we had a super week with them. We had done a bit of groundwork for their visit: a special window-display announcing their arrival and inviting folk to a list of activities; we had been to Monsieur the Mayor and asked permission for them to sing in the streets of Neuville; we had made arrangements for churches in Villefranche and Lyon to 'borrow' them for an evening each and we had invited a reporter from 'Le Progres' to cover their visit. And we prayed!

Easter Saturday the coach arrived and in no time the jumpers were off, the shorts were on and they were soaking up the sun. We, the spoiled, didn't risk removing our sweaters!

Their programme had been well-rehearsed and their presentation was really professional. At each performance, the French folk were genuinely impressed by the reality that shone through. One lady said: "I can't explain it, but you can feel that there is something real inside of them." Indeed that was true. In the open-air, people stood around and listened – and applauded!

Their enthusiasm was infectious. In Neuville, six or seven people who had stood in the town square and listened, came back the same evening to hear more. In Lyon a huge crowd stood around to watch the drama and listen to the singing. One man commented: "It's really good to see young people who aren't afraid to advertise their faith!"

And so the week passed and as the the team relaxed and became more at ease with their surroundings their programme seemed to become even more joyful. Our newcomer to Neuville, Philippe, was thrilled with it all. He was amazed to see so many young Christians all at once and could hardly believe it when we told him they were only a section of the young folk from one church.

It wasn't all work for them, however. They had a good day out in the beautiful town of Annecy at the foot of the mountains and the Mayor of Neuville did them proud, giving them an official reception in the historic Town Hall. He took them on a tour of the château and offered them stickers and fridge magnets with the logo of the town. They in turn presented him with a plaque and a tourist pack from Ireland and the day ended in mutual goodwill.

Far too soon, for them and for us, it was back into the coach for the long journey home. The week had been such an encouragement to us and our little group and we knew that the young folk too would be blessed for all that they had done.

The following week we were in Ireland for Julie and Lionel's wedding. The sun shone and the church was filled with their families and friends.

George had the responsibility of marrying the happy pair, which was lovely for him. Julie looked radiant and the newly-weds were whisked off to their reception in a pony and trap. All very picturesque. We had a very happy day with the added spice for some of us that we would be doing it all over again in May, in France! Julie had decided that she wanted all her french friends to share in ther joy of the wedding, too. Her time with the Mission was now officially at an end but we knew that they would both continue to attend our little church and be involved in its activities.

So once again our Mission team was down to two – the Crorys. We'd been here before, but this time we felt our group was well able to take on a lot of the responsibility of the work and indeed they were going to have to do that when we left them later on in the year.

Back in France, Xavier had asked us if we could find him a job in Ireland for a month or two. We had made enquiries and had found a place for him in Glenada House, a Christian guest-house in Newcastle, County Down. He was really pleased about it and prepared to leave mid-May. Before he left, he turned up at the morning service one Sunday. It was the first time he'd ever done such a thing although he had been to many of our other outreaches. The following day he came to have a meal with us and he talked at length about the service. He couldn't understand how anyone could come to know God instantaneously and we discussed with him for a long time. As he left we gave him a New Testament to take with him to Ireland. He was a lovely young man and seemed so near to the Kingdom of God. We coveted him for Christ and our prayers went with him.

A couple of months later we were on the phone with our son, Peter. He told us that Xavier had been at their home for a meal and was very happily settled in Glenada and was hoping to stay for a long term. That was excellent news; he would be meeting all sorts of Christian people there.

Xavier's mother was a lovely, gracious Christian lady but throughout her marriage, her husband had been stoutly opposed to her church-going and meeting with other Christians. He had recently been diagnosed with lung cancer and she was very concerned about him. She very much wanted us to meet him but could think of no way to get us together as he refused to allow her to invite Christian friends into their home. But she felt that the fact of our getting Xavier a job which he enjoyed just might serve to soften his attitude a bit so one afternoon she asked us round to her garden 'to pick cherries'. We spent an hour doing just that. It was hot, and after we'd finished picking, it was only right that she should ask us in to take a cool drink! Her husband was there, sitting in a chair at the window. She introduced us and he made a real effort to be agreeable. Not willing to cause any problems, we only stayed about 15 mins. But as we were going we suggested that he and his wife should come and have a cup of tea with us one afternoon. Then we left.

Odette, his wife, was so pleased that all had gone well and a few days later they both arrived at our flat for tea and chat. They stayed for about half an hour and this was hailed by Odette as a real breakthrough as normally he refused to have any dealings at all with Christians.

The following day he went into hospital to begin his first chemotherapy treatment. Apparently the cancer was quite advanced and he was a pretty sick man.

Just a couple of days before we were due to leave Neuville, we called round to say goodbye. He was much more at ease with us this time and wished us well on our travels. We chatted for a while and were even able to turn the conversation to the subject of life after death. We left him a couple of leaflets to read and he accepted them.

He was due to start his second dose of chemotherapy the following week and the third session at the beginning of August. We were going to be away until November so did not know whether we would ever see him again, but Odette knew that we would be joining our prayers to hers for his salvation before it was too late.

The last Sunday before we left was a very special occasion. It was another baptismal service but this time it took place by the river at a pretty little place called Chazay. Those being baptised were Chantal, Julie's friend who had been converted at the Relay, two of Francoise and Michel's daughters, and Raija, the Youth for Christ worker.

The weather was flawless, very hot. We held our morning service on the river bank and the sound of our singing carried clearly across the water. Several families were out for a family picnic by the river and they looked across to see what was going on. The girls waded into the river one by one to be baptised and each one spoke about her faith in the Lord Jesus and her desire to be obedient to Him.

For many of the folk beside the water this must have seemed very strange. I'm sure most of them had never seen anything like it before. For us, as church members, it was thrilling to see the tears flow and to see the reality of faith in these young lives. We all shared in the blessing that they received and it was a wonderful farewell for us as we left them.

Our trip to Peru was looming: we were to leave France on July 1st and spend a week in Cornwall with my mother first. Then on July 9th we would meet up with the Irish team who were going to Peru for a month to visit the various mission outposts and we would fly out from London's Heathrow to Paris and thence to Peru.

We had been making an effort to learn a bit of Spanish in the past few months and could now say interesting things like: "The hotel is in this street on the right." and "There are three glasses on the table." It could only get better! Our cases were packed, we'd said our goodbyes to the folk in the church and we were all ready to go. We really had very little idea of what lay ahead of us but we knew this was part of God's plan for our life at this time and we looked forward with anticipation to the host of new experiences which awaited us.

11
THE PERU EXPERIENCE

The night seemed endless! At midnight, in Paris, we had
boarded our Boeing 707 bound for Lima and as we flew on and
on, the night came with us. After nine hours of flying we arrived
at Caracas and it was still dark. Here we were allowed to get out
of the plane and walk around while the refuelling took place.
Out we stumbled, half asleep, to be met with air so hot and
heavy it was almost impossible to breathe. The walk didn't do
us much good and we were almost glad to get back into the
aircraft and the air-conditioning. On to Quito in Ecuador,
another two and a half hours. Eventually we saw the first light
of dawn in the sky and by my reckoning it was about 11.30 in
the morning! On again to Lima watching the tips of the Andes
mountains poking up through the clouds and, at last, terra firma
in the airport.

Queueing for luggage trolleys we were besieged on every
side, hands everywhere waiting to take our cases or just asking
for a handout. The whole place looked like a building site or a
film-set and there was an air of unreality about it all – maybe

because I hadn't slept since goodness knows when. The buildings we saw were complete up to the first floor, but after that nothing but steel rods sticking up in the air and piles of stones and wood just lying about on the 'roof'. We learned later that this was quite normal: people built as much as they could while the money lasted and then left the work while they saved up for the next instalment.

The journey was completed by bus: a couple of hours of jolting and shaking on dirt roads through a moonscape of barren sand and rocky mountains. Not a blade of grass to be seen, no trees, nothing green or living. Because I was so tired it seemed like a living nightmare, the road going on and on, loud music blaring on the radio, through an endless barren horror. My one thought was: 'What on earth have I come to?' Occasionally a passenger got off at a place where there were a few scattered dwellings made of wattle and bits and pieces. How could they live like that?

The sun sank behind the mountains at about 6pm and immediately we were plunged into a thick grey mist and darkness. The bus rattled on, occasionally passing a lorry or another bus seemingly with scant regard to the fact that there was a sheer drop of hundreds of feet at the side of the road. It felt as if the journey would never end, but it did, finally, and we arrived at our destination, Moquegua, to a warm welcome from some of our missionary colleagues. We fell exhausted into bed at about 8.30pm, glad to get our heads on to a pillow. We had arrived in Peru – and tomorrow was another day.

I quote from a Newsletter I wrote to our prayer-partners some weeks later:

> *"We arrived in Peru on July 9th and the whole month was a whirl of new experiences and adventures every day. Goodness, what a country! Our overwhelming*

impression was the sheer VASTNESS of it. Journeys from one town to another take literally hours in ramshackle buses which look like everybody else's rejects, on roads that would make your hair turn white. Second impression – the sheer BARRENNESS of it. Miles and miles with nothing to look at except bare, rocky mountains and sand, lots and lots of sand. Third impression – the awful POVERTY of the shanty towns which sprawl up the hillsides outside every town and appear in the middle of nowhere along the roads, as the Indian people come down from the Sierra.- just shacks made of mud bricks and sacking or cardboard cartons and straw mats. Most of them have no sanitation or electric light and thousands of families live like that all around us here.

Other impressions? – the picturesque ladies in their round felt hats and their multitudinous skirts with their solemn, brown-eyed babies tied on their backs in a colourful shawl; the ladies bringing home their one or two sheep, a goat or two and a donkey every night, - right past the school where we are living; the plazas in the middle of every town full of flowering trees and shrubs – how they manage to survive I'll never know! What else? Oh yes, the insecurity. Thieving seems to be a way of life so never take a handbag out with you, clutch all your belongings very tightly to your person, and never, never put anything down for one minute or it will be gone!

We have also learned to live with DUST. This is, after all, a desert land, and if we go out for a walk here the dust comes up in clouds from our feet. It's almost like chalk-dust, it's so fine and it gets in our clothes and our hair, we swallow it and sneeze because of it and our clothes are taking on a grey tinge. The worst bit is getting back to the school, dying for a shower only to find there's not even a trickle of water in the shower or the taps. That happens all the time.

We have seen some interesting 'fauna' eg. pelicans, who fly along the edge of the sea, just skimming the top of the highest waves; sea-lions rolling in the waters of the harbour; humming birds in all their brilliant colours and of course, real live llamas. The butterflies are extraordinary, much bigger than our European varieties and spectacular colours. The spiders are GInormous, too!

We have experienced the funny things that the altitude can do to your health and we've eaten unspeakable things like 'steam-rollered' guinea-pig and 'Picanti' which is a local dish containing all sorts of unmentionable bits of an animal, the lot disguised with very hot peppers or spices (it's best just to swallow as much as possible and ask no questions!) We've seen orchards full of orange trees laden with ripe fruit and along the river colourful groups of folk are labouring away in the fields.

We have had the joy of meeting all the missionary family here, 14 in all at the moment and some of them have been kind enough to have us in their homes for a weekend. George has had several opportunities to preach here and there, by interpretation, and the response of the Peruvian people to the Gospel is amazing. They just can't wait to be invited to accept the message and invite the Lord into their lives. There is absolutely no problem in getting a crowd for an open-air meeting; they gather round, hands held out for any literature that is being offered and afterwards are happy to sit and chat about what they have heard. It's all quite a culture-shock for us, after France!

We are so grateful to the Lord for letting us be here. It's certainly very stress-free and it's doing us the world of good. We haven't felt so relaxed for years! Each new day brings its own challenge but is always enjoyable. Getting mail is of course a special thrill this far away from everyone but the postal service is erratic and unreliable. One of the missionaries was telling us that he has just discovered that his pastor has written to him every month this year – and not one letter has arrived! So we live in hope……..."

The church-experience was different, too. Nothing ever started on time but nobody seemed to worry. The first half-hour or so took the form of 'especiales', where the folk stood up in groups or on their own and sang, very often about twelve verses each time! The music was provided by anyone who could play an instrument and some were plied with more enthusiasm than accuracy! We went to one little wooden church where the service began with the singing accompanied by just one rather uncertain trumpet. Ten minutes later the drummer arrived and joined in and then, later still a man with an accordion. They all played in different times and different keys and the folk sang blissfully on for about half an hour.

Some of our Irish friends got up to sing "Here I am, wholly available" which is a lovely piece but they had quite a struggle to keep going because the accordionist decided to accompany them, having not the faintest idea of either the tune or the timing! Seating arrangements were quite singular, too. Usually we just sat on backless wooden forms and if there was no more room, the ladies would sit on the floor with their blankets wrapped round them, some of them feeding their babies, and very often falling asleep before the service was over. One congregation had an official 'prodder' who walked around making sure that the sleepers were awoken!

I enjoyed being back in the classroom even though there were only five children in the school! We managed to do most things, like playing recorders, making papier-maché heads and painting them, going out for Nature walks, and growing a few little flowers in the school garden as well as doing the three R's. George was kept busy with the DIY, putting up shelves, here, there and everywhere and doing other pressing jobs that no-one else had tackled.

We did our washing, in cold water, up on the flat roof- and washed our hair under the same tap! Life was all very different, and much simpler. We even experienced our first earth tremor one day ; a sound like a train going by and then for a moment everything shook and that was it.

Travelling from one town to another was often a hair-raising experience. The bus drivers drove madly, refusing to let anything go past them and overtaking even when there was oncoming traffic. En route to Arequipa one day, the bus was forced to stop unexpectedly because a man had lit a fire in the middle of the road and was waving frantically. We soon saw the reason why: rounding a bend we were confronted by a huge tanker lying on its side right across the road. We would certainly have careered right into it if he hadn't stopped us. The buses were always crowded. Once all the seats were occupied, the passengers would pull down little flaps at the side of the seats and sit there, blocking the aisles and making it nearly impossible for anyone to get on or off. Very often they would bring their animals on with them, a goat tied up in a bag, or half a dozen chickens and once we even had a llama up on the roof rack!

The roads were unspeakably bad, full of craters. No street lights of course and what was more horrifying, no safety barriers and often a sheer drop of hundreds of feet at the edge of the road. It really was nerve-wracking but strengthened our Prayer Life!

From time to time George was able to travel with one or other of the missionaries to some remote village up in the Sierra. The higher they got, the more likely they were to suffer from 'altitude sickness' which is very unpleasant. On one occasion, George was driving up into the mountains. The road was awful with huge craters every few yards, so big that he had to drive into them and out again, and driving was becoming very stressful.

They stopped for a break after a couple of hours and got out to eat their sandwiches. George suddenly felt himself breaking out into a cold sweat, hardly able to remove the foil from a glucose tablet to get it into his mouth – and the next thing he knew, a Peruvian companion was sitting beside him on the roadside, taking his pulse, and the missionary was coming at a run with the oxygen cylinder! They had maybe gone up a little too quickly and George's system couldn't cope. He was all right after a rest and only had a bit of a headache but it gave them all quite a fright.

We also had our personal encounter with the thieving that seemed to be part and parcel of Peruvian life. We had only been in the country for 24hours when George discovered that his lovely new camera was missing from our bedroom in the missionary house. Apparently all Europeans were regarded as rich and 'fair game' by the less scrupulous inhabitants of the town and someone must have climbed in through the window when they saw us leave the house. That was a salutary warning and from then on we made sure that we always locked everything, doors, windows and even our suitcases, when we left our room.

George being over six feet tall was easily spotted among the five foot Peruvians and, walking down a crowded street one day, he was spat upon by a fellow in a doorway. Turning to remonstrate with him, George felt a hand in his pocket and before he could do anything about it, all his money was gone and the thief had disappeared. Things always happen in threes, we're told, and on the very last day of our time in Peru, we were in Lima.

The town was crowded and we were being pushed and jostled as we walked along. Suddenly George felt a sharp prick on his wrist and when he looked down, his watch had gone! It had obviously been expertly sliced off with a knife. He shouted, but there was no sign of the culprit. We thought afterwards that whoever had done it was probably standing right beside us in the crowd. How would we have known? Thankfully I didn't lose anything but all the missionaries related how they had been mugged or had things stolen from them. One girl even had her knapsack slit open while it was on her back, and all the contents removed!

The plumbing in the school where we were based for the main part of our stay was less than efficient, to say the least. Practically every week shower-heads fell off, the water failed completely for a few hours or the toilets leaked. The local plumber had an unfailing source of income! One night George got out of bed in the early hours of the morning and found the corridor awash. One of the other missionaries saw the light on and got up to investigate and put her feet into a couple of inches of water. Several other rooms were flooded and it was all a real mess. Going to the toilet was not a pleasant experience as no toilet paper could be flushed away as the system couldn't cope with it. So the offending article had to be put into a cardboard box or a paper-bag at the side of the loo! It's amazing what you can get used to!!

All too soon, our time in the school came to an end. The weather was getting very hot with temperatures around 32C, the mosquitoes were out in force and having a field day and our bedroom was like an oven. It was quite uncomfortable. In spite of that we knew we would be sorry to leave. It had been an amazing four months, full of new experiences. Not only that, but we had been able to really 'wind down' and that had been such a blessing.

The children and the missionaries in the school gave us a farewell party which was lovely. They had made us special cards and a couple of cakes with 'Bye' and 'Thankyou' on them in icing. I was presented with a tape recording of my recorder class – as if I could ever forget it! And we were given all sorts of goodies to eat and a couple of peruvian T-shirts. Then the cases were packed and off we went to spend our last week in a holiday home belonging to some Lutheran missionaries, right on the Pacific coast. We would spend a week there terminating in a Field Conference for all the mission family at which George would be the speaker.

The little house was lovely, built up in the sandhills above the beach. It had a swimming-pool in the garden and some bright flowers growing in profusion around the door. Preparing our first meal, we nearly blew ourselves up with the cooker! All the taps on it were broken and there was a ring with no tap for it at all that couldn't be turned off. Just across the field was a Lutheran missionary, having a well-earned break too, and he promised to come over and fix things for us. The next morning when we got up, we found everything in the fridge frozen solid! Oh dear, something else that didn't work. Funnily enough we didn't get annoyed about it – our stay in Peru had taught us to expect the unexpected! It all got fixed in the end and we had a good week.

Each day we would stroll down the path between the bushes which led to the beach. There was not a sound to be heard but the incessant screaming of the sea-birds standing along the water's edge. We saw hundreds of little red crabs who rushed out of the way as we approached. I watched one digging itself into the sand, every few seconds bringing up a clawful of sand, throwing it out and then patting it down flat before going back for the next load. We loved to watch the pelicans who skimmed the surface of the waves always in single-file and always just behind the furthest and biggest breaker. Sometimes we saw a lone fisherman up to his waist in the water throwing his net out into the waves. It was all very peaceful and far removed from our normal way of life.

The Field Council proved to be an excellent couple of days with warm fellowship and good Bible-teaching. We all got to know each other a little bit better and the atmosphere was very relaxed. We were there, wanting to hear what the Lord had to say to each of us. George spoke very well and we had two good discussion sessions.

Then it was goodbyes all round and off to Lima for us to catch the plane to take us back to France. Goodness, it seemed a whole lifetime away! We had been leading such a different existence for these few months and seen what life was like in the Southern Hemisphere. It had been so worthwhile for us in so many ways and we knew we would remember for a long time some of the sights and sounds that had confronted us.

We were to board our plane in Lima and our first impression of the city was not very favourable. It seemed very dirty, with broken pavements and dilapidated buildings, even right in the city centre. We had just arrived in the main plaza when we heard shots – it was the police firing tear-gas. People began to run to get away from it and the police water-cannons arrived, jet-spraying all around them. We had no idea what it was all about but the whole population seemed to be in tears!

The next morning we were up at 5.30 and left the hostel at about 7am to get to the airport. There was no trouble getting a taxi: there were hundreds of them in various stages of dilapidation, mostly Volkswagen 'Beetles', cruising the roads all the time.

As soon as a driver saw a 'Gringo' or a likely passenger, he would slow down and yell 'Taxi!', hoping to get hired. We got a really bad one, filthy dirty (driver included!). He opened the boot with a screwdriver to stow our cases, there was a plastic sheet instead of a back window, a 'starred' windscreen and the front windows were permanently open. The noise of the engine drowned all chance of conversation and what happened when he hit the brakes was anybody's guess! Still, it got us there and for half the price that we had paid on our arrival four months ago.

Our Air France flight left mid-morning and we were delighted to get seats beside the emergency exit – lots of leg-room for George. The meals were fantastic, almost too rich for us after four months of Peruvian tepid chicken-and-chips. After a trouble-free flight we arrived in Paris.

How quickly one's life can change: we had left 32C in Lima and now we were plunged into 3C on a cold French winter's day! We were tired and a bit frazzled after the journey but worse was to come. Our internal flight to Lyon didn't leave for another nine hours! So we sat around in the airport and had plenty of time to rearrange our thoughts and to begin to anticipate what we might find when we got back to Neuville. We wondered what we would find. How had our little church advanced during our absence? Had the folk in the church taken on the reins of the work and had it gone well? We would soon know.

12
The End In Sight

Arriving in Lyon we were almost in a stupor of exhaustion! That interminable wait in the Paris airport had numbed our senses, which were pretty well deadened after the long flight from Peru. Our hearts were warmed, though, to find a welcoming committee waiting for us. Julie and Lionel were there with three or four of the Neuville folk and they left us in no doubt that they were genuinely glad to see us. That did us good although we hardly had the energy to be very chatty on the way home. They just dropped us at the door of our flat and said goodbye, knowing that all we wanted was bed! In we went and found the heaters on, Julie's electric blanket on our bed and food in the fridge. Christian love in action!

The following evening when we were feeling a bit more human, Julie and Lionel came up to see us and hear the news. Sitting round a huge log fire, they filled us in with all that had been going on in Neuville since we had been away. It all sounded very positive: reasonably good attendances at all the activities and individuals showing increased willingness to be involved and to take responsibility in one way or another. That was great and we were so grateful to God for having kept this little fledgling church together.

Julie had news on the personal front as well – she was pregnant! Apparently she had had a miscarriage in August but had fully recovered and was feeling very well, and excited.

A young couple in our building in Trévoux had become the proud parents of a baby girl while we were in Peru, and they called up to our flat to invite us to a celebration. They had invited all the neighbours for aperitifs in their flat and we were delighted to be included. This was our 'family' in Trévoux and it was lovely to join in their everyday lives. We enjoyed seeing them all again and they were eager to hear all about our 'Peru Adventure'. Over the years we had been able to talk to nearly all of them about our faith and some had shown a genuine interest in Christian things, Some of them had accepted the Scripture calendars that we had offered them and one girl confided to me that evening that her husband never left for work in the mornings without reading the Text for the Day. So that was an encouragement.

After a week or two we began to realise that our little church in Neuville was showing signs of being more stable than it had ever been. Gradually it became clear to us that the time had come for us to begin to take a back seat. We felt the Lord was saying to us that it was time to think about getting off-side and letting the French folk take over the work. Funnily enough we weren't really taken aback at the thought. To both of us it just felt 'right'. Much as we loved the place and much as we loved the folks, we wanted to do what was best for them and we felt that if we stayed on too long, they would just sit back and let us get on with it whereas the indications were that they were now ready and willing to assume responsibility. The Lord had brought us there to do a job and now He was telling us that our job was almost done.

On Sundays we arrived to find the keyboard and guitars out and several young people all ready to play them. No more need for me to be at the organ! Samuel and Michel were perfectly capable of taking the Bible Studies and the members were showing signs of really caring for one another. There were intimations of a genuine 'growth in grace'. This, of course, was what we'd been working for all along and we rejoiced to see it.

We held our Annual General Meeting at the end of December. George had asked Samuel to preside, which he did very well, and all went smoothly. During the meeting we told them that we would probably be leaving them in the autumn of '94 – at which point dear old Madame Bos shed a few tears into her handkerchief - and asked folk to pray about the choosing of elders to take over when we left. We wanted everyone to feel at ease with the change-over.

So that was it. We had accepted that we would be leaving France and be back in Ireland within the next twelve months. What our next step would be, we had no idea but we had confidence in the Lord to work that out for us. Meanwhile there were still things to do and a few more months in which to tidy up the loose ends.

A few days later, we were spending an evening with another missionary couple, Roger and Dominique whom we had become friendly with over the years. After telling them of the developments in our lives, Roger began talking about some of the many towns and villages in the area that had no sort of Christian witness whatever. He was really concerned about them and as he talked on, we both began to wonder if the Lord was asking us to go and start off somewhere else. All he had said so far was, 'Leave Neuville' and we had automatically assumed that He meant, 'Go back to Ireland'. But was that right? Maybe it was a possibility we should explore?

In the days that followed we mulled it over, looking at it from all points of view. We prayed that God would show us clearly what He wanted us to do. He had promised to guide us, and we clung on to Psalm 32 v 8 'I will instruct you and teach you in the way that you should go.' We knew He would do it if we just waited and trusted. We eventually settled down to talking our thoughts over with the Missions Secretary at the next Field Council that was imminent, and see what he thought. We would much prefer to stay in France and use the experience we had gained than to go back to Ireland where there was a church on every street corner and hundreds of Christians!

When we discussed the matter at the Council meetings, we got the distinct impression that the Mission would not be prepared to support us in starting another work. There were no candidates for France in the offing, and the only work they would support was what was going on in Paris, which wasn't the Pioneer church-planting that we would have wanted to do. So we gathered that the Lord was saying No to that idea.

With an uncertain future ever-present at the back of our minds, we got on with life. We held a Peru Evening in the church, to which we invited all our friends. We had brought all sorts of things home with us: woven wall-hangings, wood carvings, leather coasters and pictures, sweaters made of llama and alpaca wool, bookmarks and other small items showing scenes from Peru and so on. These we displayed on a long table at the side of the room and they were picked up and examined and discussed with interest by all the folk who came. We showed lots of slides of the country, the school where we had lived, the awful roads, the barren mountains and the little churches we had visited, all to give a flavour of what it had been like. Then we told them about the life of the missionaries there and the way God was working in establishing churches here and there and we described the services, so different from our own. It all went well and we were delighted to see lots of our English class pupils there.

Just before Christmas we did a distribution of seasonal tracts in Trévoux. On our way round we called at Xavier's house to see how his father, José, was doing. The last time we had seen him was before leaving for Peru practically six months previously, when he was just about to start the chemotherapy. He received us politely but was obviously tired. We didn't stay long, but left him one of the Christmas tracts to read and he promised that on a 'good' day he would come with his wife, Odette, and have coffee and cake with us in our flat one afternoon the following week. They duly came and stayed for about an hour. We had a friendly chat, sitting around a blazing log fire, (we were going to miss that!) and we promised to call in and see him again before we left for Deputation in February. We were well aware that Odette was delighted at the friendship that was developing between us. She had prayed so long for his attitude to soften towards the things of God, and maybe this was the beginning of the answer to her prayers.

I had resumed my Bible Studies with Annie and one day at the beginning of January I was able to share the details of my conversion with her. For once, she listened carefully and I felt she was really taking it in. Finally she said: 'I know I'm not a Christian'. To me, that was good news. At last she was starting to understand the Gospel. We talked on and I gave her a little booklet which explained very simply about faith in Christ and left her to read it, praying that the Holy Spirit would open her heart and mind to realise that she needed the Lord in her life.

In the middle of the month, George went off to Perpignon with our neighbour, Tony, who had bought a house down there and was practically re-building it. George, being an exwoodwork teacher, was being pressed into service! We were delighted that they were going to spend at least 8 or 9 days together and had asked the Lord to open up opportunities for George to talk to him about Christian things. Off they went and the following day George phoned: 'We're safely here and everything's all right. You'll never guess what…. The whole way down in the car we talked about faith and believing in God and the Christian life! And at the end of it, Tony said, 'Well, that means that I'm not a Christian; I didn't think I was!'"

So within a week two of our friends had come to see the truth about themselves. But that wasn't enough: we earnestly prayed that they would get to the point of finding the Lord in a personal way. A couple of days later George was on the phone again: "We've met the folk who live in the house opposite Tony's and they're Christians!" Tony might be planning to move away from Trévoux and we might be going back to Ireland, but it seemed that God wasn't going to let go of him!

We heard from the Missions Committee who suggested that as we were going home for Deputation we might as well just stay there and make that our cut-off point. For me, the vibrations from that were just all wrong. We had planned to officially constitute the church before leaving on Deputation and we needed to make sure that everything was working out as it should and that would take time; we wouldn't even be able to give in the required three months' notice on our flat and what's more, the Neuville folk would feel that we had just abandoned them with no proper time to make our farewells. We renewed our prayers for guidance. If God wanted us to go, then of course we would but not unless He showed us very clearly. We needed to be sure.

We did decide that it would be sensible to extend the time in Ireland for a couple of weeks after Deputation so that we would be 'on site' to explore any offers which might come our way. The Committee was agreeable when we put it to them and that was settled.. After several weeks of praying about the matter, we were aware of a growing conviction that we should return after our time in Ireland, finish off all matters concerning the church which needed to be done and then leave definitively at the end of June rather than in the autumn as we had originally planned. It would be better to leave the folk to start off the new church year on their own without us there.

Things at church were going well and we marvelled to see the growing unity and increased involvement of these folk who had become very dear to us. We could well understand the affection Paul had for the churches he had planted – we felt the same. The Ladies' Group had been meeting all year with a regular 8 or 9 ladies. I was happy to be part of it and really enjoyed our times together. We met on a Tuesday morning in each others' homes. We drank the inevitable cups of coffee and the ladies talked openly about their needs, their joys and sorrows and the life of the church. That went on for about an hour and then someone would share her thoughts on a verse of Scripture and there would be discussion about what was said. The prayer-time followed, sometimes lasting another hour. There was no pressure to leave or to get finished: it was just an excellent time of mutual support and fellowship. A few years previously we could not have envisaged such a thing. God had been so good.

We were packing our cases ready to leave for Ireland in a couple of days when Francoise appeared at out door. She brought us a lovely card in which she had written how much she appreciated all we had been and done and that she didn't want us to leave without knowing it. It was really very heart-warming and as we thought of all the ups and downs we had gone through with her and with Nicolas, we thanked God for what He had done in their lives.

Our last task before leaving was to go and say goodbye to José. It was obvious that he was getting weaker but he talked quite happily with us and once again we were able to talk about life after death and how it was possible to know that we were right with God. We had never been able to talk with him so openly before, and we knew that God was beginning to open his heart. We didn't know if we would see him again but we hoped he would still be there when we returned for our last few months in France. We would be praying for him.

That night we held a very special meeting in our centre in Neuville. The object was to officially and formally constitute our church. This was the culmination of all our years, of all our heartaches, of all the joys we had experienced. The meeting went well with all our most-involved folk present, 20 of them. We started off with a time of praise and thanksgiving to God for bringing us to this important moment. Many of the folk voiced their gratitude to God in prayer and the singing was heartfelt and joyful.

Then came the Business Session and Michel got to his feet and explained all the requirements of French law that we needed to fulfil. All the necessary papers were in order and the folk voted them in one by one. Next, the voting-in of the Elders: Michel and Samuel had been the obvious choices and they were accepted by all present. The last official duty was to collect all the signatures of the Foundation Members of the new Eglise Evangelique of Neuville. With that done, there was a feeling of delight and relief among us all We'd done it! Or rather, God had done it. He had built His church, only a little one but it was there, a new candle shining in the darkness of central France. How often we had wondered if this day would ever dawn and now here it was and our hearts were full.

So, at long last, the church we had come to France to plant was well and truly planted and in two days' time George and I would be going back to Ireland for our last tour of the churches who had so faithfully supported us. Would the Lord show us the next step while we were home? We had no inkling of anything in regard to our future but we knew without a doubt that God already had it all planned out for us. We just needed to find out what it was.

13

The Final Lap

We spent ten cold, windy weeks in Belfast – a longer time than usual to give us the opportunity to explore a few possibilities for our future. One or two churches had made a few tentative approaches but nothing had come of it and we were no wiser as regards our future than we were before we left France. The Lord had firmly shut the door on each slight opening so we still knew nothing of His plans for us.

During our long absence, the little church in Neuville had experienced tragedy with the deaths of two young people connected to our families. One was Annie's ten-year old grandson who had drowned while swimming in a river. The other was the 19-year old son of a couple who had just started attending our services and he had been killed in a road accident. The church had rallied round and it became everyone's concern to help and comfort. Michel and Samuel, the two elders, seemed to have taken their responsibilities very seriously and the church was functioning very well under their leadership.

We had left 14C in Belfast and in Trévoux it was already 25C, so it was straight into T-shirts and shorts! Our little garden was an absolute jungle so we worked in it on and off most of the first few days we were back. I couldn't help thinking: 'It's hardly worth all this effort; no-one will bother to look after it when we leave', but there was no way we could ignore it.

Tony and Carole gave us a warm welcome back and informed us that they too would be leaving Trévoux in the summer. Tony had bought another old house down near the south coast (14 rooms!!) and they would be going to live in it. So the building would revert to the French; Katharina and Matthias were already back in Germany.

As the time drew near for our departure, it seemed that lots of folk wanted to spend time with us. It was lovely, but made the thought of leaving them even more painful. Michel and Florence called up for coffee one evening. Arriving at about 9pm, they didn't leave until 2 o'clock in the morning! We talked about the church and about their involvement, about the way they envisaged the future; we heard all about their family and what they were up to – all five of them! We talked and laughed and just enjoyed each other's company. Thinking back to how prickly they had been when they first joined us we rejoiced in the change in them: no doubt we had changed too. God had been at work in all our lives.

As the days went by and the weather got warmer, I began to find that increasingly I was dreading the thought of having to leave this lovely place and all our friends and go back to Ireland. I had begun to feel so much 'at home' in France; the language now came easily without having to think about it; we had such good relationships with the folk we lived beside and we had come to love the little church in Neuville, and I did not want to leave it all. There were all sorts of things that I was scared of going back to. The 'Troubles' were ever-present with the bigotry and hatred that raised their heads around us; the weather wasn't good (and I loved the sun!); and somehow I knew I would miss the reality that we had found in our little church. God had become so real during these years in France: every day we had looked for opportunities to speak to someone about our faith and somehow it wasn't like that at home. I was afraid of slipping back to an easy, comfortable Christianity that didn't make many demands. It wasn't an inviting prospect and I began to get really depressed about it. I was saying to folk all the time that we were trusting the Lord to work out our future and that He knows what He's doing but that didn't stop me living in dread of it. The more I thought about it, the worse it got until it became a burden almost too much to bear. I knew my attitude was wrong and dishonouring to the Lord but I couldn't seem to get out from under it. Eventually, when it was just getting too much to bear, I poured it all out with tears to George. There wasn't very much he could do or say to help me, but the outpouring was a relief and consequently I began to feel better.

The following day was a Sunday. George was leading the service and Samuel was preaching and both seemed to speak directly to my need. I had to obey the Lord. I had to believe that He wanted the Best for me, and I had to trust Him to give me the grace to cope with whatever happened. It was a matter of 'Lord, I believe; help my unbelief.'

Just a couple of days later we were off to spend a weekend in Vallorcine, a little village practically on the Swiss border. The weather was beautiful and the scenery was breathtaking. We had been invited by the lady whose son had been killed while we were away. She was a very new Christian and wanted to spend time with us talking about her faith. As is happened, it didn't work out that way. They were having all sorts of alterations done to their chalet and the place was full of men carrying planks and hammering and generally doing what workmen do.

It was nearly impossible to find a quiet corner or indeed to have any sort of conversation.

So George and I were left to enjoy the place on our own. One day we walked across the mountains into Switzerland and arrived at a tiny railway station called St.Bernard, - with huge posters of the dog all over the place. A train was standing at the platform; a little white train with pictures of St.Bernard dogs with their brandy kegs under their chins painted on the carriage doors. It was really quaint, and with the backdrop of the mountains, it was like a living postcard. Spending half a day up in the mountains was a real blessing. God's creation is awesome! And as I looked around and marvelled at the beauty I realised once again how mighty God is and how incredible that the God Who created all that could be bothered with the details of my life. How dared I even think of being rebellious! He loved me and He knew what would be good for me and I had only to obey.

The wonders of the natural world had always spoken very loudly to me: the rainbow against a black sky, the restlessness of the ocean, the immensity of the skies and the clouds which are constantly changing, the beauty of the flowers and trees and the amazing variety of the animal world. This, apart from the Bible, was where I could see God most clearly. These were the things that lifted my spirit. I had always felt a real kinship with Wordsworth, my favourite poet. He was thrilled by creation, too:

' My heart leaps up when I behold
A rainbow in the sky…….'

David, the Psalmist, was another kindred spirit: 'the heavens declare the glory of God…' and now, at Vallorcine, I had been caused to acknowledge God as the great Creator, and felt that He was at work in my heart again. The weekend passed quickly but my thoughts had done a turn-around and I went home with peace in my heart.

For the next couple of days, my Bible readings were full of assurances of God's care and that He was in control of my life. I still didn't want to go back to Ireland, but the panic was no longer there and I could live with that.

At the end of May, we had our last Church Weekend with the folk, in a beautiful old château surrounded by parkland. For the first time, we two knew nothing of the planning and we were tremendously encouraged to see the spiritual input, and it was good to see our non-Christian friends taking part in the discussions and obviously feeling quite at ease in the group. There were about forty of us with a dozen or so children. It rained a bit but there was still enough sunshine for us to get out and play games and to have the inevitable barbecue. It was a good time together and everyone seemed to enjoy it.

Back in Trévoux we went and said a final goodbye to José. We knew we would probably never see him again and he knew it, too. He seemed to be much more open this time and George was able to have a really good chat with him, urging him to ask God to forgive his sin and come into his life. He listened but made no comment. It was sad to have to leave him without knowing whether he would come to faith or not. We had begun to feel that we could be friends.

On June 10th, the church held a 'Soirée d'Adieu' for us. This was their official goodbye. They invited everyone they could think of who had known us and 60-70 people came. There was no set programme; people came and went all through the evening, and many were the good wishes for our future and the regrets at our leaving which were whispered into our ears. Dear people, all of them. We had been privileged to have known them.

A buffet was laid out and folk stood around and chatted. Finally Michel stood up and 'did the honours'. He made a little speech and, on behalf of the church members presented us with a beautiful painting on silk – (Lyon had been the capital of the Silk Industry)- and a series of videos called 'Life in France'. This had been a fascinating series on the television, highlighting traditional crafts and looking at some of the little hidden villages where life hadn't really changed much over the years. I had loved watching it and how the folk had found that out, I have no idea. They couldn't have given us anything that would have given me more pleasure.

The last few days were flying by and we were invited for meals here, there and everywhere. Our relationships with folk seemed to be closer than ever and we realised just how many good friends we had made. Folk called up to the flat to say goodbye: Xavier, home from a year in Ireland, called up twice in the last week to say his farewells! We were given little presents and some lovely books but at last it all came to an end and it really was time to go.

Packing began in earnest. Out of the store came the tea-chests and the boxes and cartons. Down came the pictures and the ornaments, curtains were washed and packed away, our hundreds of books and CDs and videos were boxed up and labelled. Cupboards were emptied and the flat began to look stripped and bare. The removal van was due to arrive very early on June 24th. George would leave with it and I would stay behind to clean the flat and get it ready for the 'état de lieu', which being interpreted means ' the state of the place'. Most tenants dreaded it- it was a visit by the landlord who examined every wall and doorframe and floorboard to see if any damage had been done. Woe betide anyone who had drilled holes in the walls! It had to be in as pristine a condition as the day it was let, no stains, no marks, so I had to make sure ours was perfect.

Incidentally, I reckon it's an excellent practice which Britain would do well to adopt! No more grotty apartments!

Our final day dawned. ..... at a quarter to five!! We heard the beeping of the lorry as it reversed up the drive and no sooner had it arrived than the loading began. The piano caused a bit of a problem and had to be lowered over the wall because our outside steps were very narrow! Fortunately Tony and Lionel arrived to help at about six o'clock and it was 'all hands on deck' for a few hours as we watched all our worldly goods being stowed away in the depths of the van. In the end there wasn't another inch of space left and we had to give away our garden furniture to the neighbours! It was all done by eight o'clock and I waved George off down the drive as they started on the long trek back to Ireland.

I hopped into Tony and Carole's flat for a welcome breakfast and then it was back to the flat to sweep and clean up. There wasn't really very much to do and the landlord duly appeared about half an hour later. I followed behind him as he went from room to room. He was a hard-headed businessman and not a very popular figure in the town. Most of the tenants didn't like him much but we had always got on all right with him. I did feel a bit nervous though as I watched him ticking off items on his checklist. The inspection only took about an hour and a half instead of the usual three or four! But happily he found absolutely nothing to complain about and was tremendously impressed. He even assured me that our deposit would be repaid in full! That didn't often happen. So, that was good and that was it. The flat was locked and I retreated to Carole's for lunch.

I was to sleep at Julie's house that night and then fly out early next morning. I knew they were away for the day at a Jesus Rally in Lyon so I spent the rest of the day in the garden. It was very hot, about 31C. I lay on the grass for a while, staring up into the blue sky and thinking about the happenings, the highs and lows and all the good things that had happened to us over almost nine years. We were definitely very different people from the couple that had arrived in Paris for language training. It had been good, very good. The afternoon was long: I wished it would go on for ever! I went for a last little walk round the town but it was too hot to go far.

At last Julie and Lionel arrived, full of enthusiasm after their march in Lyon. We spent the evening chatting and reminiscing and then it was time for bed. I slept surprisingly well and didn't find it difficult to get up the next morning at five o'clock to head for the airport. Quick goodbyes were said, a couple of kisses on each cheek and that was it. Over. Finished. End of an era. Adieu, la France! Hullo again, Northern Ireland – and another leap into the unknown.

•••

Footnote: A few weeks after our departure we learned that José had died but that he had become a Christian before the end. What a thrill!

For us followed a year of unemployment and waiting. There were difficult times, but God faithfully provided for all our needs. Eventually George received a call to the pastorate of a Belfast church and so our new ministry began. But that's another story.